THE WASHING ROOM

A Story of Stories

By My Ngoc To

The Washing Room
Copyright © 2013 by My Ngoc To

All rights reserved. No part of this book may be reproduced or transmitted in any form or by any means without written permission from the author.

ISBN   978-0-615-79135-7

Printed in the U.S.A.

To my family, for loving me.

*"When you hear a dirty story
wash your ears.
When you see ugly stuff
wash your eyes.
When you get bad thoughts
wash your mind.
And
keep your feet muddy."*

—Nanao Sakaki

NOTES TO THE READER

Before you go on, I should tell you a few things:

- The names of certain people and institutions have been changed out of respect for their privacy and concern for their safety, though I'm not going tell you which ones they are.

- I am not a doctor, and my experiences and observations should not be used to diagnose yourself or anyone else with mental illness. I write this with the sole intention of sharing a story that I think can bring hope to a lot of people.

- Life doesn't have to suck, and you are not alone. If you think you feel the sink, ask for help. Try it, you will be amazed at how many people care.

- I love my family, even when they are mean.

- This book has a happy ending.

INTRODUCTION

QUESTIONS

"Bé Bưởi bị bỏ bú ba bốn bữa Bé Bưởi bưồn."

— Something my family used to say

[Father] "A new home and a new school? Isn't it a bit scary?"
[Chihiro] "I think I can handle it."

— Scene from *Spirited Away*

MS. WILSON PULLS OUT THE ugly brown mat and asks me what my name is.

"My Ngoc," I say.

She squints her face. She does not understand.

Of the three daughters, I am the only one without an English name. My oldest sister, who is twelve years older than me, is called "Nhung" at home and "Julie" at school. I call her "Chi Nhung" though since she's older than me. Chi Ti, my middle sister, is seven years older than me, and goes by the name of "Kelly" in American settings. At home my family calls me "Buoi," which means grapefruit because when I was born I was as pale as the grapefruit flower. Since I wasn't starting school right away when we came to America they held off on assigning me an English name, and by the time I went to preschool, I was

2

still My Ngoc, only with with an Americanized pronunciation: "Me Knock."

Ms. Wilson starts writing with her Sharpie. She stops and asks me if my name has a hyphen. I don't understand what she is saying either. It's my first day in preschool and everyone here is speaking weird. My lips seal shut in fear. I nod my head. She responds by drawing a small line between the two syllables of my name: "My-Ngoc," and tells me to use this mat whenever we have naptime.

Today I don't feel like sleeping. At first I make farting noises with Joseph until Ms. Wilson tells us to stop. He falls asleep soon afterwards, and I am left alone to think of other ways to amuse myself.

On my left side I can see the teacher playing solitaire at her desk, which is laid against the back corner of our classroom.

I feel lonely. I wonder if she feels lonely, too.

I wonder if she knows I am awake. Probably not. Still, I try my hardest not to make any noise as I roll around from side to side in search of a comfortable position. Eventually I curl up in a ball and face towards the right, away from the teacher.

Joseph is already snoring. His little belly rises up and down, up and down, and behind him are twelve other children, whose bellies are also moving to the rhythm of sleep. Not knowing what else to do, I play with the wrinkles on my sleeping mat.

An idea comes to me. On the count of three, I suck in as much air as I can and hold my breath until it feels like my lungs are going to burst. My head grows warm, and I can see a million tiny silver stars dancing on the ceiling. Just when the stars are about to fill my vision, I find myself letting it all out and taking in new gulps of air.

I try again and again, sucking air in, holding it, watching the stars appear, and feeling my chest hurt. Perhaps if I try hard enough I can actually die. My vision is just about to explode with stars when lights come on. Naptime is over, and I have to hand in my mat. I tell myself that I will be able to do it next time, but before I know it, preschool is over, and I am still alive.

My parents never wanted me to die. In fact, they did everything they could to keep me alive. But death had been tugging at me since before I was born. I almost slipped out of my mom when she was two weeks pregnant with me. She was working at her shop when she felt something wet come out between her legs. She ran away from her stand, where she was selling fabrics, and retreated to a corner to check her underwear. There were pink spots.

Scared that she would lose me forever, she hurried to the village doctor and asked him what she could do to save me. From his tattered chair in his fly-infested office, he pulled out a dirty pill container from his desk, gave a handful of them to my mother and said, "Here, this should do it."

My mom did what she was told, but the pink spots persisted in coming. After two days with no improvements, she rushed to her friend for help.

"What doctor did you go to?" her friend said.

My mom replied, "The one in Long An, the local one."

"My God! No, silly, you need to go to a real doctor, like one in Saigon." She handed my mother the name and address of someone she knew and told her to leave immediately.

My mom was too scared to ride her bicycle there, for fear that I would slip out from all the motion, so she hitched a motorcycle ride up to the city.

Once she arrived, my mom explained to the second doctor, who was a lady that time, what had happened and how the medicine was not helping at all. "Hand me what you're taking," the doctor said. My mom pulled the few pills she had left out of her purse and gave them to her.

The doctor laughed and handed them back to my mom, "This is Vitamin E, dear. You've been taking Vitamin E!" She kept on laughing again as she grabbed some needles from her cabinet. Without much explanation she injected my mom at the top of her thighs with some clear fluid. Whatever it was, it worked—I came right back up, like a little yoyo.

That first battle was over, but there were many more to come. Each time, my parents would be more and more unequipped to help me. By the time my depression became debilitating, my parents were already worlds away, for the word "depression" does not even exist in the Vietnamese language.

My battle with death had its origins long before my breakdown, long before its first whispers shook the walls of my fetal home and tempted me to wither into darkness. The tectonic plates of my life had started shifting long before my parents even met each other, gathering up a silent tension that would someday explode on that late October night so many years later.

My grandmother's could not have died at a better time. Right after I turned one, my grandfather, who came to America by boat and established himself working for a refugee resettlement organization in Atlanta, wrote my mother a letter saying that he could bring us over to America.

There was one thing holding my mother back: her mother, my grandmother, who would not be crossing the ocean with us. The thought of leaving her frail and lonely mother to live in solitude for the rest of her life kept my mom from going through with her decision, and so the letter just sat on her desk for months, opened and waiting for her reply.

Though, as with many major decisions in life, the choice had been made for us without our knowing. A final shift in the underground plates of fate brought fortune our way. On May 15, 1993, a few months after the arrival of the letter, a kitchen accident caused a pot of boiling water to fall on my grandmother, killing her on the spot.

The next day, my mom wrote her response to my grandfather. By September 18, 1993, my parents had sold the house, closed the business, signed off the paperwork and exchanged teary goodbyes with all of our family. We took one last family photo in a field of bright yellow flowers behind my uncle's house. The sky was a bright blue that day. We boarded the plane to America with our freshly made passport photos, and my parents bid farewell to Vietnam.

I was only one when we left. I had no time to think about death—I was too busy getting used to flying. Whenever I whimpered in the seat, my mom panicked and brought me to the lavatory, where I played with the toilet paper rolls, giggling and swatting and smiling because the paper was flying everywhere. My mom twisted the paper back onto the roll, then I repeated my game, and we did this until I fell asleep and my mom deemed it safe enough to return to our seats.

For the first month we stayed at my grandfather's house. This gave enough time for both of my parents to find jobs and earn their driver's licenses. The night before our departure, my step-grandmother handed a jar of old frying oil to my mom as our final parting present. It had the history of all meals ever cooked in that home for the past month, and had the recollection of burnt meat and black flakes which rose up whenever shaken. My step-grandmother and all of her children, who began life in America with a more privileged background, would continue to shun our family for years to come.

When the thirty-first day of the month came, we packed our bags and moved to a crumbling apartment in Clarkston, a neighborhood inside the metro Atlanta area saturated with immigrants and refugees from all over the world. Our tiny apartment had cockroaches and leaking ceilings. The carpets were heavily stained with all sorts of human matter. My sister's nose bled. I got a skin infection from rubbing my fingers against the carpet whenever I was bored.

With both of my parents working and my sisters enrolled in school, we had to find some way of taking care of me while everyone was gone. My parents paid the old woman and her daughter who lived beneath us ten dollars a day to watch over me. That worked for about a month until her daughter found a new job, and they left the apartments, left Clarkston and headed towards that mysterious place where refugees go when they find something better. After that, my parents turned to the old man who lived beside us. Unlike the previous woman, he had no children and he spent all his days inside the house smoking. He was the Cigarette Man, and his house was the Smoke House.

I spent my days inside his nicotine-scented walls while my mom chopped up vegetables in a hotel kitchen. In the evenings, when my sisters dropped me off at home, she practiced painting nail polish on plastic fingers as she studied for her nail license. Talk had gone around that the nail salon business was the only way for Vietnamese people to make any decent money. If my mom did not try something new soon, she would be spending the rest of her life washing dirty hotel sheets or cutting carrots in a kitchen alongside racist coworkers.

In Vietnam, she also dropped one job for a riskier, higher paying one. She grew up thinking that she would be a schoolteacher, but after one year it became clear that such a meager pay was not enough to provide for her family. Instead she sold fabrics in the underground market, contrary to the will of a government that disliked private enterprises. She was caught and put in jail twice, but every time she got out she traded even more textiles. Within a few years she had become the most popular fabric vender in the district.

My dad, on the other hand, did what he was supposed to do. It was in his blood to abide by the law, even if it meant having a lower salary. When he came to America he worked at a paper-cutting factory. Every morning saw him stepping out of our apartment in the same outfit: a tucked-in collared shirt with a small hole or two hidden in the armpits, faded dress pants, and a belt to keep his pants from slipping off. The clothes were all from Goodwill, just like his lunchbox, made from blue and white plastic that frayed on the edges.

My dad was a good worker who arrived on time and never made trouble with the other employees. Eventually, they promoted him to a management position—instead of working in the assembly line, he watched over the cutting machine, an amalgamation of a steel arms and a huge guillotine blade that could slice giant cylinders of paper into bits.

One day the machine broke, and he had to fix it.

While he was poking his hands in and out of the machine, something released that was not supposed to release, and the blade fell. It sliced off the tips of his four left fingers, cutting cleanly through the bones of the first metacarpals. What remained were bloody stumps with blue, shriveled skin at the tip and glistening bits of bone.

For several months right after the accident, my dad stayed at home to heal. The doctors managed to take flesh from his thighs and sew them back on as fingers. My dad had his fingers back, and I had my dad back. We no longer needed a babysitter.

During the day my dad and I sat on the limp floral couch and watched whatever was on public broadcasting. There was not enough money to buy new videos, so we watched the same one over and over again—a cartoon about a duck and its adventures running on the road. Sometimes my dad would set me on his lap and let me pound on the keys of our small electronic keyboard, also from Goodwill.

My mom worked fourteen hours a day to pay the extra hospital bill, which came on top of rent, gas, electricity, and feeding a family of five. We were living down to every penny. If my mom spent a dollar on lettuce, she wrote that dollar down in her spending book. Sometimes she snuck back little spare chocolate snacks left behind by the restaurant. Help also came from a myriad of small corners. Our neighbors, who worked as cashiers at the local farmers market, rummaged through the boxes of rotten apples that were about to be thrown out every Tuesday and picked out the best ones for our family to eat.

My dad ached to do something for his family, but he had no way of earning any money, not even a quarter. At times, he would prop me on his shoulders, and we would go out into the parking lot to go hunt for coins. And there we were: an old man and his little girl, both insane and clad in grey, hunched over and looking for pennies left behind by those blessed with jingling pockets.

After his surgery my dad did not want to go back to the factory. The only option left was to join my mom in the nail business. At first he worked as a regular employee, performing basic manicures for customers. Once, he sat down to do a manicure for a young lady, but when he lifted his hands to begin, she recoiled, screamed, got up and left without a word. After that incident each fingernail that he trimmed felt like a blow to his pride, though he never uttered a complaint.

Once he resumed work, I went back to the Cigarette Man. The days passed by with the same silent routine: first the gray of the bleak mornings, and then a deep blue in the evening when the sun set on our neighborhood.

At this time the kids would come outside to play. Badminton rackets swung everywhere, little games of freeze tag filled the streets, and children ran around chasing fireflies. Most of the kids were older than me and wouldn't let me play badminton with them because I was too short. But I watched. Sometimes my sisters and their friends played cards at our house. I couldn't join them because I was too young to understand the rules, so I hid behind the couch and listened to them laughing, fiddling with my thumbs as silent tears slid down my cheeks.

There was one friend I could play with though. She was fat and mean, but it was better than nothing. Once I made a duck out of pastel colored Legos. I was proud of it. I shared it with her because no one else was around. We sat on the curb as the sun baked our skin. She wore red shorts, and me green. I sat on her left staring at the empty parking lot beneath our apartment. We didn't talk much. *I* didn't talk much—I never did. But I had managed to share my duck, and that was special. Our lives during those apartment days were only bad in retrospect. Back then we could ask our neighbors for sugar at any time. Our world was lit with an enchanting azure simplicity that didn't seem precious when we lost it years later.

When the last bit of blue light of the evening faded to black, our parents came home from their factory jobs, and we went inside with them. On some nights my dad would sit on the patio outside our apartment and smoke with the neighbors. It was so magical, the way smoke just appeared out of nowhere, and I asked my dad if I could try. He handed me the cigarette. I put my lips to it and tried blowing, but no smoke came out. I handed it back, disappointed and confused at how grownups could put so much time into nothing.

In the morning the colors changed again. My dad walked me down the peeling metal green staircase, and after one flight we reached the front door of the Smoke House once more. I don't remember much about the place—only that inside there was a door that swung out from the hallway and towards the kitchen, and it was behind this door that I would hide behind for hours. When my sisters picked me up, they would kiss my hair and tell me I smelled like cigarettes.

During all those months, I stayed fixed behind the door, sensing only the smoke that drifted around my skin, unaware of all that was happening, all that was yet to happen. My parents were living on their continent of immigrant life in America while my ground split apart from theirs—without realizing it, I was soon standing on my own island of American dreams. The rift between us made me more incapable of seeing their love over the years, and death grew more confident in its advances.

We have enough pennies now—it's time to leave. My parents have saved enough to buy a small nail store half an hour away, and that is now our future. We move into a small suburb of Atlanta called Lilburn. Our new neighborhood has a completely different makeup. Instead of tan, browned faces, we see only pale white families. Instead of going to preschool, I enter the third grade. Instead of going to the Cigarette Man, I become my own caretaker.

Once, when going home from school, I fall asleep on the bus and miss my stop, so my bus driver takes me home last, after she drops off the other kids. It is a long drive and she talks for most of it. Towards the end she asks me what I plan to do when I get home.

I suddenly think about how wonderful it feels to be clean, especially after a long day of school. I imagine hot water splashing on my head and clear blue shampoo lathering away all the dust and dirt from the playground. I imagine opening the shower curtains and seeing my bathroom mirrors fogged up from the steam and the heat, and suddenly I want to take a shower right then and there. The bus is so hot, and my clothes are dripping with sweat from my hour-long ride. I know I'm dirty and all I want is to be clean. I want so badly to tell her everything, but I can't.

I don't know how to say "shower."

My cheeks turn red. I hang my head trying to think of the word, but, after a long pause, when it still hasn't come to me, I lift my head and say, "I wash myself."

CHAPTER 1

THE WASHING ROOM

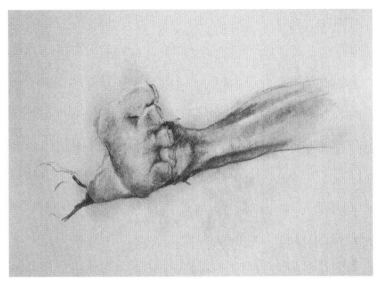

Foreshortened Foot (2012)
Graphite and Charcoal on Newsprint
18 in x 12 in

"Truth, like gold, is to be obtained not by its growth, but by washing away from it all that is not gold."

—Leo Tolstoy

"The purpose of art is washing the dust of daily life off our souls."

—Pablo Picasso

I'VE ALWAYS WONDERED what kind of a lifestyle it takes for people to grow fungus on their bodies. I used to think that these people were the exception, but I have touched too many feet with clumps of dirt scrunched up under the nails to continue believing that the majority of the population keeps itself clean.

I especially love thick, yellow toenails hiding years of bacteria between layers of keratin. Heels covered in calluses. Toe hair. Sores. A fine layer of dead, crusted skin running from the heels all the way up to the knees.

This is the world of a nail technician: flakes of dead skin and cuticles, bits of nails and hair and dirt squished into balls nudged into the corners of spa chairs. Anything that can get filthy will grow filthy, and three years of subjugation under this law has taught me to wash my hands.

In the back of the salon, behind the television, in a dingy room lit by one fluorescent bulb, nestled in the corner between the heaters and the water fountain, is a small room equipped with a toilet and a sink. There are little decorations as well: a plunger, a scrubber, and a dusty fake plant that has claimed its territory on top of the paper towel dispenser for ten years. There is also a mirror above the sink. It is covered with toothpaste, grease, and spit: every imaginable form of human matter. A sign above the door reads "restroom" for all those who desire to use it as such. I never pay much attention to that sign; to me, it is the washing room.

It all started with two bags. When we first bought the nail store we didn't have enough money to buy a washing machine, so we just brought all the dirty towels back home with us. Every night, my dad hauled home these sacks. Whenever I heard the garage open, I ran downstairs to greet him at the door.

Sometimes I helped. I handed him the towels, three at a time, and he arranged them in the washer so that the weight was evenly distributed. Most of the towels were only slightly damp, but on occasion, I would pluck out a sopping wet one covered in slimy green mucus—the special Aloe Vera scrub that we smothered over people's legs in a deluxe pedicure.

Other towels had bits of hair—perhaps from the workers—or pieces of of nail or skin that had latched on during the pedicure. I cheered every time my hand picked up a clean towel.

Afterwards I washed my hands and helped my mom cook dinner. My parents ate quickly. Twenty minutes was more than enough to finish a few bowls of rice, enough time for one cycle of the washing machine. Once we finished, I scurried to the laundry room and helped my dad unload the towels into the dryer.

In the morning, I'd go downstairs to see a pile of fluffy, white cotton towels on the kitchen floor, each one folded in half, arranged into piles, and fitted into a bag that was squarely tied at the top. At 9:30 my dad would come down, pull the bags through the door, and head off to work. Then I'd stare at the door for a few seconds as the garage grumbled onwards and into silence.

The nail store was the family business, and as a result, the entire family was affected by it. My two elder sisters had to march to work when they were in high school. They called it war, and working at the store simply meant killing off as customers as quickly and efficiently as possible. My mom called them up to duty whenever there were not enough troops to handle the army. It was always at an unfortunate time:

Buoi you want to go to the park? We are downstairs, putting on our shoes, about to step out the door when the phone rings. My sisters look at each other, smiles dropping. Do we pick up? Should we pick up? Do we dare? The phone stops ringing and guilt rushes into our hearts, mixed with feelings of joyous liberation, and we tell ourselves it's ok if we spend one day at the park. But then the phone rings again and this time we know we cannot escape. Sorry Buoi we'll have to go again another day. They leave for battle and I stay at home and climb onto the sofa again.

Days like this passed by gradually, almost imperceptibly, until suddenly, it came my turn to go.

At the nail store I eat three times a day: once in the morning before I go to work, once six hours later when I'm at work, and again when I come home. At the store, I eat between customers. I finish one pedicure, run to the backroom to microwave a bowl of instant noodles, and then return one pedicure later to slurp down the entire bowl in five minutes. I have to because customers are waiting for me outside.

If my mom doesn't see me within five minutes, she will call the intercom and scream for me to run back up, "The customers are squirming in their chairs—grab their feet before they can leave!" The moment I finish my last noodle, I sprint to the bathroom and wash my bowl. Sometimes I am in such a rush that I accidentally spill the broth or I leave soap marks on the mirror, but I don't care and I don't have enough time to wash it off because I have to go.

My mom manages the store but doesn't want the employees to think that she is favoring the daughter, so she lets them have first pick in customers. All the clean, polite, considerate, and generous guests are divvied to workers according to their seniority and skill. I have no experience with acrylic nails, waxing, or any other service beyond the basic manicure and pedicure. I can only rub feet and squeeze hands. I only know how to cut people and scrub their parts. What does that make me? I am left with a splendid selection of customers ranging from the dirty to the impolite, the indecisive to the cheap. At times, I find all these traits in a single customer.

Like the lady whose nails I labored over for two hours. Each of her toenails had to be the exact same length and shape; a millimeter off made her scream in protest. She glowered over me the whole time I cut her cuticles, squirmed at the lightest suggestion of pain, and, when I scrubbed her feet, made me scrub them again because a spot on her heel still felt a bit rough. Her legs were fat and heavy. I tried lifting them up to massage her. She saw me struggling and didn't even make an effort to help. She wanted white tips on her toenails, which meant that I had to paint a thin layer of white at the edge of every nail and then take a brush and meticulously thin them into the perfect shape. She asked for a design. I gave her the design. She made me change it twice. When I did it for the second time, she leaned forward to inspect it, made a face, and then said, "Oh whatever I'll just have to live with it."

She ended up not giving me a tip. When my mom came to see my work, she apologized to the customer, "Please forgive this girl—she is new." I'm cleaning up as I listen. My mom continued, "I won't charge you. Tell you what—I'll redo the pedicure for free." My mom never looked at me.

I rinsed off the tub, grabbed my basket and went to the restroom, where I washed my face, and then stayed there until my eyes were dry and white again.

It is another day, a Tuesday. My mom tells me to do a pedicure at the first spa chair. I go to the back and grab my basket, two towels, and a pair of gloves. Up front there is an old black man, probably in his late fifties, soaking his feet in the tub at the foot of his spa chair. I ask him how he is, and he replies, without looking at me, with a single nod. Trying not to think about his silence—perhaps he didn't hear me—I put on my gloves. When my mom sees that I am getting ready for pedicure, she comes over and, without saying a word, gives me a mask to put over my nose. I give her a quizzical look. She sighs and says, "Just use it."

I put on the mask and ask the man to lift his feet from the now murky water. They rise up from the whirlpool bath like two sea monsters: huge and brown, covered in scales and barnacles and disease. I look at my mom. She meets my gaze firmly, and by the look of her eyes I know that I am to stay quiet; that, although this pedicure will take me three times as usual to finish, it will cost as much as the basic pedicure; that she is giving me this pedicure because none of the employees will touch his feet.

There are four basic parts to a pedicure: shaping the toenails, cutting the cuticles, scrubbing the calluses, and massaging the leg from the foot to the knee.

His toenails are a quarter-of-an-inch thick. They have the texture and hardness of wood and sprout from his toes, growing so long that they eventually curve inwards. He has a fungus, and it makes his nails turn green in some areas and purple in others. The man avoids eye contact.

I have to think of a way to cut these trunks of toenails into stubs. I find my answer in the cuticle cutter, a pair of scissors with short, chubby blades. It is smaller than the nail clipper, but its blades are far enough apart for me to cut down his nails. I work on the little toe first. It takes me dozens of cuts to whittle each nail down to size. I make sure to cut them as short as possible—right down to the skin, so that no filth can accumulate underneath his nails. Little pieces of skin fly out, and I duck as they nearly hit my eyes. Even while wearing the mask, I can smell the bacteria on his skin.

I finish fifteen minutes later and move onto the cuticles. Most people clean cuticles around their nails, which makes it easier to tell what's cuticle and what's tender skin. But this man's cuticles are so thick that they grow in layers, forming a white gelatinous wall around the sides of his toenail. I'm terrified that I will cut flesh instead of dead skin.

Nevertheless, I cut, feeling my way around by judging the softness of what my blade is touching—if it is too elastic, I know it is living skin. Suddenly I see blood spewing from the rims of his toes.

I have cut people before, and every time I apply a clotting solution that makes the blood dry. After I treat the wound, I look up at him, but he appears oblivious to it all. At first I think that he is just very tolerant of pain, but then I realize that he has lost his ability to feel any pain in his toes; the bacteria under his nails had long ago killed the nerves in the skin, so the cuts and wounds and festers on his toes are completely unknown to him. I am glad that he does not notice my shivers.

Now comes the part that I dread most: the heels. The whole time, his feet lay completely flat on the towel. I ask him to raise his feet up and prop them on their heels. He does, and in doing so reveals an entire topography of canyons, plateaus, and rivers that run the length of his foot—a landscape made completely out of dead skin, dirt, and calluses.

I am trembling and fighting the urge to cry. I grab the callus remover, a liquid that, when applied to the bottom of the foot will dissolve the layers of dead skin and calluses. I lather his feet in this substance and then wait five minutes as it eats away the dead skin. When it is finished soaking, I get the razor and shave away his calluses. A small mountain of brown foot flakes forms on the floor beneath his feet.

Scrubbing time.

I scrub, and I scrub, and I scrub.

I lift his feet into the air and scrub every single nook and cranny of his foot. I scrub the sides of his toes, I scrub around his toes, and I scrub between his toes. By the time one foot is done with, the dissolved, dead skin has accumulated into a fine layer of mucus that covers the entire pumice bar. It's so slimy that I can't scrub anymore; in order to finish the procedure I have to get a new bar.

Thirty minutes later, I go onto the last part of the pedicure: the foot massage. But first I have to wipe off the chemicals so they won't keep eating his skin. If the chemicals sit on the skin for too long, the customer comes back with a lacerated, bleeding foot and a less than cheery attitude. So I make sure to clean them well and then place his feet back into the tub.

Something immediately feels strange when my hands touch the water. My fingers are wet, but I am wearing gloves. I pull my hands out of the water and spot a hole in each glove. They are both dripping wet with pedicure broth. I check the box of gloves, but there are none left.

Keeping the ruined gloves on my hands, I wince my way through the rest of the pedicure. The massaging part is not as difficult as it is grueling. I want to give this man a good pedicure, but the more I touch him the more I want to run away from him. His legs are hairy and his skin so dry that the lotion cannot absorb, and I have to rub it off with a warm towel afterwards. Usually the massage lasts only five minutes, but his goes on for half an hour. By the time I finish, the towel is brown.

The man stays quiet for the entirety of our session. Is he mad at me? Did I do a bad job? I wait for him to leave the spa chair so that I can clean up the tub. But he doesn't. Instead, he leans over and slips me a five-dollar tip.

Later on, my mom tells me that he never tips.

I put the five into my pocket and clean up the mess. I throw away the pumice bars covered in dissolved skin, sweep up the piles of callus on the floor, scrub away the thin line of brown bubbles that dried to the walls of the tub, throw away the towels, sanitize my tools, pick up pieces of toenail that have flown across the room, and, when all of that has gone, I retreat to the bathroom and wash my hands again and again and again.

The days go on like this from the eighth grade, when I did my first manicure, to when I graduate from high school. I work from nine in the morning to ten at night, six days a week, every week that I am not busying myself with school. The store closes at eight, but I leave several hours later because my mom takes in late customers. Even if she doesn't, there are the stragglers—people who come in ten minutes before the store closes and then ask for a deluxe pedicure, which takes an hour to do. It is usually nine-thirty when the last customer leaves. However, I have to stay and help clean up. It's what the new employees do. I have to wash the windows, sweep the floor, wipe down the spa chairs, put back the nail polish, rearrange the chairs, and dust the tables.

There are times when I feel like collapsing, and my only desire is to go back home and sleep. Food doesn't matter anymore. I only need rest, and if I have enough energy, I will shower. Then I remember that I still need to mop. For a moment, I can only hang my head and look at the pile of hair and dirt and nails and tissue at my feet. I feel so tired all of a sudden—small, weak, and beyond belief. But then I lift my head and sweep the trash into the bin. I move on, smiling to myself, because I know I can still plan out my mopping so that the last place I arrive at is the washing room.

CHAPTER 2

LITTLE TIGER

Lightning (2012)
Chalk Pastel
9 in x 12 in

"I have always believed, and I still believe, that whatever good or bad fortune may come our way we can always give it meaning and transform it into something of value."

– Herman Hesse, *Siddhartha*

"The soul is healed by being with children."

– Fyodor Dostoyevsky

A SIX YEAR OLD GIRL wearing bright yellow shorts and a pink polka dotted shirt is sitting on our couch. She's staring at the carpet. Today is my first day in the eighth grade and her first day in America.

When I come closer, she opens her mouth to say "Hello," revealing a set of crooked yellow teeth with extra canines sprouting from the front. She was born in the year of the tiger, and these are her fangs. Despite this, there's something quite cute about how she speaks so little and keeps her head down most of the time. Her head, shaped like a square, is almost as big as her torso, and her hair sticks out in little tufts behind her head. She took her first plane ride two days ago and made it all the way across the world.

This is Na, and I am going to take care of her for the time that she and her mom need to live with us. I first met Na three years ago when I went back to Vietnam with my family in the fifth grade. At the time she was just a pudgy square-headed toddler. Since then, her mom had divorced her dad and married a family friend who lived here so that she could get a green card to America. Their wedding took place in Vietnam, and I remember receiving photos of the two and wondering if they were in love.

Na is too young to know what is going on. She can't comprehend how far Vietnam is from America, and how big the ocean is that separates her from her dad. She doesn't understand why her mom needs to go to America. At the airport, when saying goodbye to her father, she forced herself not to cry because she didn't want her dad to see her sad.

I take to my duties immediately and teach her the alphabet. When she can more or less pronounce the syllables, I move on to teach her simple words. We sit for hours on the carpet of the computer room rolling around laughing at her mispronunciations. Then I teach her all about time: how to read the analog clock, how to say the different months of the year, how to count days—whatever it takes to cover the year of kindergarten that she missed.

My kindergarten teacher used to count with the class the number of school days that had passed. Every morning she would go over the weather, time and date and then ask what number day it was. I was really excited for the 100th day, when our school would hang up banners all around the hallways and bake dozens of cakes for us to eat during lunch.

When that day passed, I panicked. What was going to happen next? Numbers didn't go over one hundred, so would that day even exist? That was the closest thing to an existential crisis I would experience as a child. The next morning I came into class and waited for what seemed like century as we went over the weather again, and then the day of the week. My breath almost stops when we get ready to count the number of days. "Please don't pick me, please don't pick me," I prayed. She called on someone in the front.

"One hundred and *one!*"

"That's great honey!" said my teacher.

All of my fear and anxiety was gone, and I just felt silly. "Oh," I thought. "Well that was easy."

Now that I'm going over numbers with Na, I need to teach her this as soon as possible so that she can answer the question if her teacher ever asks her. "What comes after 100?" I ask her.

"Uh... one hundred and one," she says, without wonder.

"Yep," I say. "Yep. Good job." After that I decide that she is set on her numbers.

During the summer before ninth grade I take her outside of the house as much as I can. We go to the pool together, and sometimes I invite my friends to come with us. I haven't gotten my driver's license yet, so we walk. Luckily the pool is just across the street. After we get back I cook a meal for both of us: stir-fried egg noodles with bits of broccoli and carrots and shrimp. Na eats it all. She tells me it's her favorite meal.

And then, one day, I come home from school to find Na, sweet little Na, sitting on the couch with her big square head hung low on her shoulders. When she sees that I'm here she turns her body way from me. I ask her if she wants to go to the pool, but instead of jumping up she stays silent. I try asking several more times, but she gives no response and then starts sniffing. What's wrong Na, what's wrong? She doesn't answer, and I think I know the reason why but I wait for when she's ready to talk about it.

Sometimes I find her lying in bed staring at the wall, doing nothing, saying nothing, and I ask her what was wrong. She gives me the same silence and then lets out tears. The whole time I know she is also crying out of shame, because she is not supposed to let anyone see her cry. I look at her and I see my younger self—we both grew up crying alone.

"Na, what's wrong?"

She can hardly answer because her nose is too stuffed. "My, my dad," she says. Sniff. "I miss my dad."

I try hugging her, patting her back, staying quiet, but her tears keep coming. The more I talk, the more she shrinks into herself, until she appears just like a tiny, hurt animal. Still, I persist, "Na, your mom had to come here. She came here for you, so you could have a future, and you know that." My words make no difference. They cannot go past the pain that had formed a shell around her. We're in the same room but living in our own universes, haunted by our separate pains.

In the following weeks I make an effort to spend more time with her. Sometimes, if we're in an adventurous mood, we take on the twenty-minute walk to the library. If the house is short on groceries to make the stir-fried noodles, we go and get produce from the Kroger next to the pool. I spend time with her and she spends time with me.

One day I crack. During our walk home from the grocery store, I see a group of kids I know from school walking towards us. I'm not close to any of them, but I recognize one of the kids. His name is Adam, and he lives in the first house on the right from the entrance of our subdivision. He stands for the relaxed and insular American life that I wish for but will never have.

I suddenly become very aware of the coffee-colored Kroger plastic bags dangling from the edge of our palms.

They are coming closer. I wonder if any of them also have to take care of a little girl with horrible teeth and a sadness that no child should have to bear. Probably not.

As we pass each other, I avoid eye contact and pretend not to be embarrassed. We cross the street back into our neighborhood, and the moment they disappear from sight I feel safe again. I don't tell Na any of these thoughts, but I think she knows. She's knows a lot for someone so young.

I want Na to have a normal childhood growing up with me, but this will never be a reality for her, or for anyone in a family under the nail business. Right now, I am all that she has, and whether or not I like it, she is my responsibility. So through her elementary school years I continue to take her to her to school events and attend parent-teacher conferences in place of her mom. Chi Ti had done this for me in the past, and now it is only right that Na gets the same treatment.

Soon I cannot separate her from my life. If my sister is home on the weekends and we go to the movies, Na will be present. At every concert, every party, every pageant or family outing or dinner, she shows her face. Na has developed a semblance to a tumor baby that grows out from one's shoulder—it is not possible to be happy with it present, but sawing it off would end up killing the baby. I feel everything for her. I hate her at times and love her at others. I want to take care of her, and another part of me wants to abandon her. I try to keep these emotions contained, only letting them go in my diary, but Na still knows, as she always does.

One day I find a letter stuck under my bedroom door. It is written on wide ruled paper torn out of a composition notebook. Irregular, scribbly handwriting fills the page, the handwriting of a third grader:

> *I'm sorry that I've ruined you and Chi Ti's life. You guys have been the best to me and I'm sorry I did not treat you better. I promise I'll stay away and not bother you anymore.*

She signed her name and placed her inked thumbprint at the end as an official mark.

Na is gone now. She ended up living with us for five years. During that time she graduated from elementary school, got braces, took piano lessons under my teacher, and then moved out during the summer before my senior year of high school. Now I come home and find the house silent and sterile. The TV sits useless and still, and the coffee tables are missing their abandoned bowls of rice, which used to always get left behind by those little hands. I am lucky to be so busy with projects and tests and college applications to keep me from thinking too much, because the truth is I really miss that girl.

My parents often tell me that every person we meet comes into our lives for a reason. Because of the way karma and reincarnation work, we either have some connection in the past life or we are meant to make a connection in this life. Perhaps I owed Na something in my past life. Perhaps she had once been my little sister, and I failed her as an older sister. Whatever the case, after five years of living with her, I can't deny the fact that she has given me just as much, if not more.

CHAPTER 3

THE KNIFE

Transcriptions in Time (2009)
Graphite
12 in x 18 in

"...time was not passing...it was turning in a circle..."

– Gabriel Garcia Marquez, *One Hundred Years of Solitude*

A month after my eldest sister gave birth to her last son I came by her house to see how she was doing. I found her in bed breastfeeding her youngest son. It looked as though she had just woken up from a nap because the sheets were rumpled, her hair was tousled, and her shirt was pulled back from turning in her sleep, revealing a small triangle of skin at her stomach. We talked, and at some point during our conversation she saw me looking and lifted her shirt up to reveal the entirety of her stomach. "Buoi, do you want to see what happens when a woman gets older?"

It looked like a balloon that had been inflated to its fullest state and then left to slowly deflate on its own, with wrinkles and dents and strange craters all over its sides. Stretch marks covered everything below the ribcage, and a hideous scar ran across her pubic line, the result of multiple caesarian sections. The skin sagged. It sunk down the base of her pubic line. This was all the extra skin that her body had no use for after giving birth to three children. There was so much skin that when she clenched it with her hands, blobs of skin rolled out from between her fingers, like linguini oozing out from a pasta roller. After her pregnancy, the skin accepts its unnecessary role for the body and, on its own, willed itself to die—it turned brown, the color of rotting bananas. She told me she was thinking of getting a tummy tuck.

At first I revolted at her decision to get plastic surgery. I think anyone would if they knew the details of the operation.

To perform a tummy tuck, surgeons make three incisions in the body: a smile along the pubic line extending towards the hips, a frown below the rib cage, and a circle around the belly button. They cut the frowns and the smiles so that the edges meet each other, making an eye on the stomach. This eye encompasses the areas of excess skin that will later be removed. The belly button is set free by the incisions surrounding it, so that it will not be ripped off from the body when the skin is removed.

After these first three cuts are made, they take a pair of clamps and peel off the skin from one corner of the eye. It's kind of like peeling the chicken skin off of your chicken wings, except it's a slightly more difficult because the skin is still alive and clings to the muscle throbbing underneath. You notice that human fat is yellow and clings to the skin in tumorous clumps. It hangs everywhere, like gelatinous stalactites dripping blood, like villi from the walls of the small intestine. All of this is removed. It gets sucked out with tubes, cut away with knifes. And a considerable amount just comes away with the skin.

You see that muscle is pink, not red, that its sinews run in parallel grooves. Blood sometimes gets stuck inside these grooves and clot, forming brown puddles. It looks as if someone threw embers onto the stomach, turning the flesh to ash in areas where the skin was burnt the most.

The eye is then removed completely. When the surgeons lift it off the body, it looks like some sagging hide taken off of road kill. It looks human. You know it is, but it's so hideous that you wish it wasn't.

To finish the procedure, they pull the flap of skin above the gaping hole down, over the bellow button, until it meets with the bottom lid of the eye. They skin is held in place as they suture the flaps back together. Finally, they locate the bellybutton hiding beneath the skin and cut a hole around it yet again, so that it can reappear. To finish the operation, they secure the bellybutton with a few last stitches.

That, all of that happened to my sister.

A couple of months after the surgery I see her at one of our cousin's wedding. She's wearing a cream-colored dress that she hasn't worn in six years, not since she got married and had kids. The dress is floor-length and has small ripples of fabric that run across her torso and emphasize the curves of her body. Her waist looks tiny, and from the side, her stomach lay completely flat. Seeing how great she looks, I am quite happy about her decision, and I'm sure her husband is too. I tell her how fantastic she looked. She smiles sheepishly and said, "Oh come on. It wasn't like I exercised or anything."

When Chi Ti got her nose job, she spent two weeks in bed. She couldn't move because the pain from her cuts also migrated to other parts of her body, and she was slightly too warm the whole time. Her face was swollen and splotched with the colors of dying flowers: mustard yellow, mauve, and faded violet. I had to get ice pads from the freezer and press them to her face to help the swelling go down. There were bandages and cuts all around the base of her nose, and they bled. I played a sick game where I pretended her face was melting, and random parts would fall off unexpectedly, and it was my job to keep them in place.

I think it was because mom called her ugly all the time. It didn't matter that looks didn't matter. Every time they met, my mom would criticize my sister's nose and tell her she has the exact same face as our ugly aunt. Sometimes she would apathetically joke, "Your nostrils are so big you'll never be able to be rich. Any money that you find will just slip right out of them." It was kind of true. Out of the three sisters, Chi Ti was the one who spent her money most lavishly on clothes and perfumes and purses. Her closet was stocked with towers of shoes and once-worn gowns. It didn't matter that her boyfriend thought her nose was cute. It didn't matter that she won a beauty pageant. It didn't matter that my mom was just joking the whole time. It didn't matter because the jokes carried some sliver of truth, and it killed my sister.

Though of course I didn't know how much it killed her until she told me late one night that she wanted a nose job, and I told her she was ridiculous and stupid and stayed up all night trying to pull her pack. But then I looked at her. Something in her eyes had already glazed over. I imagined her body being cut up into pieces by my mom's words and reassembled into a different person by some cold doctor, and I saw that my sister had already chosen to go down this path, and I cried.

Before Chi Ti's rhinoplasty we all came with her to the office before her surgery. Now my mom and I are waiting in yet another room as nurses shuffle around us. They wear heels and tight pink shirts emblazoned with jewels that spell out "BOTOX" over their over-sized breasts. The receptionist flashes us her abnormally white teeth and greets us with a face powdered with thick, matte make up. All the nurses carry similarly sculpted faces. They maintain eternal smiles, even as they talk, and they carry their speech with a certain quality that is almost too soft and sweet, like preserved cherries. I help my mom fill out the paperwork and translated some brochures into Vietnamese for her. We pass the time by flipping through albums of Before's and After's, page after page of shrinking bellies and tightened skin.

One of the nurses comes and escorts us to the screening office. We enter a small room decorated to be as inoffensively as possible. A large mahogany desk occupies the center of the room. On top of it sits a large computer screen set to a solid blue desktop. There is a bookshelf, a full-length mirror, and a few green plants on top of the furniture, as well as some certificates and paintings of flowers. Everything appears painfully normal until you take a closer look and see the breast implants lining the shelves of the bookcase and the giant examination chair in the middle of the room.

We sit down in leather chairs, and the prettiest nurse with the BOTOX shirt sits down in front of us. "So, uh," she pauses to look back at the papers, "Ms. Kim, can you tell me what type of services you're interested in?"

My mom conjures up her best English and explains that she wanted a facelift, tummy tuck, and perhaps eyelid surgery. The nurse smiles. Her teeth shine through like fangs.

She sets up a few videos on the computer and then excuses herself from the room. My mom and I go through the videos. They each take us through a step-by-step methodology of both tummy tucks and facelifts.

To get a facelift, they make a long incision running from the temples that first runs to base of the ear and then veers backwards, stopping at the hairline behind the ear. This makes a pocket in the face. The surgeons pull up the skin, disconnecting it from underlying tissue, and scrape away any excess fat within the hole. Once done with the fat, they close the hole and pull the skin back to the ears. The excess skin is removed, and the wound is closed. Sometimes, when there is a significant amount of fat underneath the chin, they will also make a small cut at the base of the chin and suck out the fat from that hole. In cases where there is too much excess blood, surgeons leave a drain in the wounds to suck up the blood that may clot.

We learn that she will be bruised badly for weeks, and that blood and fluids may seep out unexpectedly. We also learn that she might lose the ability to smile.

The nurse comes back and asked us if we had any questions. We don't. She smiles again, sweetly mutters some cordial nothings, and then leaves.

The doctor comes in shortly after and introduces himself. He said some cordial phrases and asked us if we had any questions. We have a few questions. My mom asks him about neurological dysfunction, to which he replies that these cases almost never happen. She asks if he can also do a brow lift and eyelid surgery.

I watched him scan my mom's face for a few seconds. His eyes gave two quick glances over her eyebrows. "All you need to do for the brow lift," he says, "is cut a small line above the temples along the hairline and then pull the skin up." The whole time he is taking a pencil and lightly sketching patterns in the air above my mom's face. He sighs, "Yeah, it's pretty simple—and to be honest it's not that necessary in your case."

After that we don't have any more questions. It is time for the prescreening. He asks my mom to sit on the examination chair. She is short—only five feet and one inch tall, so it is a bit difficult for her to get on. She slides into the chair and waits for the doctor to come. I watch her sit and wait and look at him in anticipation. No one speaks. The doctor kneels down a bit to match my mom's height and then probes her face. He places one hand on her chin to guide my mom's face up or down, left or right, and with the other prods and pulls back the flaps of skin on her face. After a few minutes he was done.

"So in your case we will have to cut behind the ears and at the base of the chin. She doesn't need that much on the face. Just a bit of work on the chin should do it, and she doesn't have that much in the first place," he says. "Here is a really extreme case on an elder lady who could not have surgery on her face. We just made an incision on the chin, and it still had pretty solid results."

He grabs a Before & After album from the bookshelf and shows us pictures of an extremely old lady who got a chin tuck. Before, there was so much fat beneath her chin that she literally had no neck. Afterwards, it was all gone.

My mom is very impressed.

Our surgeon then explains to my mom that he can now examine her for the tummy tuck. "I'll come back in a few minutes. For now, you can undress." He handed her a white smock that opened up in the front. 'Wear this, and you can keep your underwear on."

When the door closes, my mom slowly takes off her clothes. Bit of fat lay resting on the tops of her thighs, around her arms, and at her waist. Her stomach swells out a bit, and it has a few stretch marks and scars in its face, the aftermath of carrying four children. After she finishes undressing, she wraps the smock around her body and climbs up the examination chair. This is the first time I am seeing my mom this naked. She looks so soft. Her skin is pale and almost translucent, and I can map out her veins on her feet, which dangle off the chair as she stares expectantly at the door.

At last, the doctor comes in. My mom opens her smock, exposing her little white belly, and the doctor begins his examination. After a few minutes of silence, he explains that my mom will be getting a medium tummy tuck. "Again, it's not that bad. After the surgery, we could reduce it to about half. You'll definitely still be able to tell the difference though. The results will still be good. As for the rest, we can't get to it because it's located behind the muscle frame. But she can easily fix that by losing—maybe five founds. Your mom is not that big, and that should do it." With that, he shakes my mom's hand, exchanges polite somethings, and then leaves. My mom scurries to the door and put her clothes on. She doesn't look at the mirror as she passes it.

The last person to see us is the manager of the clinic. I am speechless when I see her. Perhaps she thinks her beauty stuns me; perhaps she's gotten the same reaction many times and mistakes repulsion for attraction.

Her body had been cut, sewn up, altered, covered, pulled, twisted, and inflated in almost every possible way: a nose job, breast implants, facelift, hair-dye, heavy make-up, heavy gold rings on three fingers, Botox, and a tummy tuck. She is almost sixty years old, but packaged to be twenty. She looks neither old nor young, yet she doesn't have the sort of ageless beauty that some women as they gather as they age when they manage to carry their gravity with grace.

It is as if her taut, flawless skin will snap at any moment and spew out her contents. She turns out to be an amazingly sweet lady though, and an excellent businesswoman. She had been a patient at the clinic for sixteen years before she became its manager. Her surgeon is our surgeon. As she talks to my mom, I imagine maggots sprouting from her nostrils. I expect her body to erupt and expose the true contents of her body: her fatty, morphed innards. It isn't hate that I feel for this lady—it is pity.

She hands us the papers. The tummy tuck will cost $6,000, and the facelift either $8,000 or $11,000, depending on whether my mom chooses general or local anesthesia. "Do you have any more questions?" the lady asks, smiling.

My mom wants to see her scars. The lady stands up and shows us her belly, and we can see a thin scar at the pubic line where they had performed years ago. Then she bends down and shows us the scars on her chin and face. My mom's eyes light up when she sees how faint they were.

We leave after that. In the car my mom asks me, "Wasn't that lady pretty?"

I don't say anything.

"What did you think of the surgeon?"

I pretend not to hear. It is hard to drive because all I can think of is the doctor's hands molding my mom's bare skin. Each time they move, it is as if a tiny blade is tearing its way deeper into her stomach. I see her sprawled on the operation table, cut up cleanly, with skin flaps dangling over the sides, covered in clotted blood and fat. I look at my mom. She is looking at me. I say nothing and keep on driving.

CHAPTER 4

COLLISIONS

I Am Exuding Happiness (2012)
Ceramic Head with Raku Glaze
10 in x 12 in x 13 in

"Love consists in this, that two solitudes protect and touch and greet each other."

– Rainer Maria Rilke, *Letters to a Young Poet*

Love is an act of collision, when two bodies come together and react. When things go well, a mutual bond will form between the two. They can keep their entities constant while remaining attached. A healthy relationship takes the form of two stars colliding and fusing their orbits together, forming a binary system, in which they dance around a shared gravity.

When it comes to collisions, many things can go wrong. In milder cases the two objects will drift apart. In some cases, both things will explode, as it did with us, in a series of smaller explosions that tattered our core to bits.

There are other, rarer, but considerably more horrifying cases, in which one objects travels at such high speed, and is so much more massive, that it will devour the other. In these cases, the lover most feverishly and madly in love will want to eat the partner. One such collision almost came to completion five years ago.

It is Monday, December 7, 2008. The Texas police run into the home of Christopher Lee McCuin to find him sitting at the kitchen table getting prepared to eat dinner. He has an ear boiling in the stove and a chunk of raw meet on his plate with a fork set neatly beside it.

Upon seeing the police enter, McCuin bolts towards the door and manages to escape from the house. The police chase him down shortly afterwards.

McCuin had put much preparation into preparing his food. The meal was caught on Friday when he asked his girlfriend, Jana Shearer, 21 years old, to discuss some matters regarding their relationship.

When the meeting ended, McCuin beat her repeatedly with a blunt object. It only took a few collisions for her to fall dead to the floor. After that he spent the weekend further mutilating the body, carving out pieces out of various parts of the carcass.

After an entire weekend of work, he felt a sense of completion and went to seek out his girlfriend's mother. "I want to show you what I've done," he said. She followed him into the house, after which he prompted her to look into the garage.

The mother put her hand to her mouth, and ran screaming out of the house to find a policeman. The interval had been enough time for McCuin to set up his last act.

Perhaps McCuin had carved out even more pieces from the body after she left. Maybe he already had the pieces sitting in the fridge. Perhaps he knew that he did something that he should not have done. But the collision had already happened—the reaction was already in full speed, and all he had left was to bring it to completion. Either way, the story remains the same: he never got to finish.

There is a predator in every ecosystem, and when it comes to chemistry, water is like a piranha. It is designed to rip apart whatever it lays its hands upon. Two hydrogen atoms are posed like guns on one side of the oxygen atom. With their slightly positive charge, they will stick to any sort of negative charge. The oxygen, which is twelve times more massive than hydrogen, floats like a giant of negative charge. It is drawn towards any positive molecules in the vicinity. With just three atoms, the water molecules are fully equipped to tear apart both spectrums of charges.

But water never acts on by itself. Rather, it hunts in packs.

Take, for example, the disassociation of sodium chloride in water. This molecule is simply one sodium atom bound with a chlorine atom. The sodium carries a negative charge and the chlorine a positive charge. The moment this molecule comes into contact with the aqueous environment, the water molecules swarm the foreigner and prepare to attack. The ones on the chlorine side reorient themselves so that the hydrogen molecules bond to the negative charge. On the other side the oxygen atoms stick to the sodium ion.

In an instant, everything is set.

The horror begins. With their teeth clenched on the skin of its prey the water molecules pull apart in opposite directions, tugging until the carcass is ripped in half. The remains float off in the water, and the water molecules move on, satisfied with their meat.

More than seventy percent of our body consists of this water.

We are carnivores.

Of all the senses, touch is by far the most intimate, for it is the only sense in which the process of sensory acquisition causes our bodies to change. Or, perhaps, it is better said that it induces the greatest degree of transformation in our bodies.

The least penetrating sense is vision. Light is simply hitting the eye. The process becomes a bit more penetrative with smell. Little bits of what we our environment enter our noses, and some particles binds to the appropriate pore in our nose, the tiny hairs in the inside are pushed to an angle, triggering a neural response. The same applies to taste, in which tiny hairs in our taste buds are responsible for sending a nerve impulse. Sounds are perceived when the hairs in our inner ear vibrate to the sound waves.

But this is all very superficial. It's simply hairs moving or bones vibrating. The actual shape does not change.

Now take touch. We are able to feel the world thanks to Meissner corpuscles, tiny oval-shaped organelles. They are located everywhere in our bodies–underneath the skin, on the linings of internal organs. Whenever our bodies come into contact with another surface, the corpuscles in that area compress and immediately fire back signals to the brain, as if information is being squeezed out of them.

When our bodies are still, there is no contact, and the Meissner's corpuscles in these areas lose their sensitivity. They stiffen, become less responsive, and eventually stop working.

When we finally do give them the stimulation they were designed to have, they immediately light up and joyously send electric pulses to the brain. Similar to how glow sticks only glow when they are bent, our bodies slowly light up as we move each individual body part. After a full session of stretching, every part of the body has been stimulated: the internal organs have massaged each other, and bone and muscles are twisting and turning and rubbing, as if reciting an old song thought to be forgotten. By the time we have finished using the entire body, we are glowing.

Every action as an equal and opposite reaction. A transaction happens when two things touch. That is why newborns that go for too long without being touched will die. That is why we can tell if someone is alive or dead just by touching them. It is through touch that the body becomes alive. If we stop moving, and stop interacting with the world, the body will forget that it is alive.

In the movie *Perfume*, Jean-Baptiste Grenouille is overtaken by love. Born and abandoned in a fish market and raised in an orphanage, he grew up as a strangely detached boy with a superior nose, which led him to seek the best of aromas.

One night, he smells something particularly beautiful and follows the scent until he finds its source: a redheaded maiden selling strawberries in the local market. He follows her, unable to resist.

He startles her and tries to quell her screams with his hands. Having never touched or being touched by anyone in his life, he clenches her neck too hard and kills her. She falls to the floor. He touches her again, but she is not alive. He smells her, but the smell is gone.

From then on, he can think of nothing but that marvelous odor and seeks to create the finest perfume in the world. After seeking the apprenticeship of a local perfume maker, Jean uses the perfume boiler in the basement to extract oils from various objects. First, it is roses.

But even with the finest flowers, he cannot find satisfaction, and doesn't even come close. So he experiments. First came the cats. But then, one by one, the girls from the town disappear. Naked bodies of beautiful women appear around the city. The bodies are not physical touched in any way except for the fact that the hair is gone.

It is this hair that Jean uses to extract the finest scents.

Overtime the town is flooded with the fear of a serial killer. Jean continues flees from the city and goes to the country to work in a perfume factory with better scent preservation technique. The journey takes many days, and on his way there, Jean discovers that he has no scent of his own.

Once there, he continues to kill in secret and eventually obtains the perfect prey: a most beautiful redhead whom he believes will bring forth the magic scent. By that time, however, the town has found him as the murderer and will hang him.

Right before his hanging, Jean takes the perfume from his pocket and lets a single drop fall into his skin. The scent expands like an atom bomb in the air, and the town is stunned by the heavenly smell. A calm, golden spray settles on the citizens and they advanced into a massive orgy. Skin touching skin touching skin—the people are engulfed in love and forgive Jean for his murders.

The perfume has given him the power to rule the world, but Jean still has no scent. Without a scent, he has nothing to give to the world and can never be loved. He heads back to the fish market where he was born and sets to end his life. He pours the perfume over his body. The nearby crowd is surrounds him and devours him, piece after sweet-selling piece.

All the love in the world—condensed into a single collision.

CHAPTER 5

THE CORPSE

Portrait with no Light (2010)
Acrylic on Canvas
20 in x 26 in

"He who fights with monsters should look to it that he himself does not become a monster. And when you gaze long into an abyss the abyss also gazes into you."

– Friedrich Nietzsche

"Out of the blue and into the black."

– Neil Young

I HAVE SEEN DEMONDS in my dreams.

There are no windows; only a light that shines bright enough for me to notice the bed leaned against the back wall of the room. Everything is covered in stains. As I come closer, my vision clears and I see that there is a lump in the middle of the bed. The lump grows in size. It rises up in the air, causing the sheets to slide back and reveal a few strands of long black hair sticking out from something even blacker in the shadows. The black thing moves. It jumps, twists, writhes itself to the side. The sheets fall off completely to reveal the face of a woman. She has blue skin, skin that has no blood in it. Her matted hair hangs down to the floor and wraps around her feet in tangled knots. Slowly, she turns her head upwards and opens her eyes.

What I see next I will never be able to forget. The thing does not have eyes, only black holes where the eyes should be. Inside of that darkness, something evil stares right through my heart. The woman opens her mouth and screeches something silent yet horrible. I am pushed towards the bed, and I watch the wide black hole loom closer and closer until the blue light has completely faded and I am completely swallowed by her mouth. The last thing I remember is the impenetrable darkness of her eyes, and for less than I second, I see that what pure evil looked like. And then I am gone.

It is October of 2010. I am a freshman at Harvard, and I am having nightmares. It's true: I am not prepared for the transition to college. I have shifted from the small, warm conservative shell of Lilburn to the ice-cold and liberal city of Cambridge. My environment has changed from mass-produced suburbia to soaring ivory towers. The people I meet are daughters and sons of presidents, with last names that match those on the buildings on campus. I tell my friend I wrote a good essay and that I got into the *Harvard Advocate*, the oldest college literary magazine in the country, of which T.S. Eliot had been a member, and he replies by saying how he has already written a book. I share my love of science and then find out that my other friend won the international INTEL competition in high school and now has a planet named after her.

The school system I grew up in had taught me to compare myself to other students, though I never thought much of it because the system always placed me on top. With this mindset still engrained in me, I only feel envy at Harvard when I see my friends' accomplishments—and then shame for doing so. I want to do everything, be everything, reach for everything, and do not know how to stop. Harvard has too many opportunities, too many stars, and I feel like a clump of floating dust in this strange, stellar universe.

It doesn't help to talk to my parents on the phone. "What are you studying," they ask. I want to study art. "Anything but art," they say. I want to study English. "Anything but English," they say. I don't know, I don't know, I'm still figuring it out, maybe Economics. "You need to figure it out soon," they say. "Because college is not cheap and money doesn't come easily. Some parents are doctors and they can sit in an office, but we are nail technicians and we have to sweat over feet and hands to live. So you need to do well in school and decide what you want to do now, because you can't go to Harvard and then graduate and have a low-paying job. It's too big an investment."

I'm too afraid to tell them about the overwhelming confusion, angst, and fear. There's no way they can understand what I'm going through. I can't let them know that I'm weak, so I tell them everything is fine, just fine. I want to stop this terribly cycle, but I can't, and now there is a hole in me.

Somehow I become preoccupied with death, and soon I cannot escape these thoughts. I try to do yoga more often, anything that can keep me from falling apart. Twenty minutes a day. Twenty minutes every Sunday. Despite these attempts I feel something awry deep down, a sense of doom, because the whole time I can't help but think of how my favorite yoga pose is the corpse pose.

It's not just because it is the easiest, but because of the feeling that overcomes me when I move into it. After a session intense yoga, shifting legs and doing headstands, lapsing into the corpse is like the most blissful surrender of all. I feel this ache in my lower back, but it goes away the moment I lie down and take a few breaths. Soon, my body just becomes numb and all the stress of my limbs that had accumulated during the session just seeps into the ground. I imagine roots crawling up through the ground and curling themselves onto my limbs. They suck the red things out of my body, the negative energy and tensions. I imagine my body enclosed by a cocoon of these roots. Once the cocoon disintegrates, I am a vessel of blue, and nothing more.

In mid November I walk through the old, historic yard to go to class. Trees line the paths; ancient branches from the opposite sides grab for each other and twist themselves into a ribcage for me to walk through. Watching the trees shed their leaves is like watching a human body decay. The orange turns to red, which, after its most brilliant display, breaks apart until all the blood has gone out of the body and there is nothing left but a bare skeleton, still clutching onto the framework of life that once was. Sometimes, I couldn't help but imagine corpses hanging from the branches. Something was terribly wrong.

Then, I have another nightmare.

I receive four letters in the mail. They come as little post cards, each with a handwritten time and place on the back. I remember holding them with my left hand. They spread out like cards in my hand, and I can clearly see information fitted perfectly into tables on each letter. I go to where these postcards instructed.

The first place is a hotel bedroom. I don't remember how I get there. There are four bunk beds in the room, one in each corner. The frames are made out of oak wood. On each bed lies a sleeping child. The mother stands in the corner reading a magazine. She has brown hair to her shoulders, and her children glow in their sleep. I don't think the woman sees me though. In fact, I don't think any of can see me—Not the mom, not the children, and definitely not the man who runs through the door with a hammer and grabs the children one by one out of their beds and cuts their bodies to bits. When the walls are covered in strips of meat and blood and the man hammers the woman to her death, and he still doesn't see me. It's a red blur and now I at a large gymnasium, somewhere I have never been before, and again, I don't remember how I got there. The gym is about three stories tall with white ceiling and white walls. A spiral glass staircase runs through the middle of the building, and I am standing right in front of it. The same thing happens again. The women on the treadmills don't turn their heads when I walk past them, and neither does the man who runs up the stair case and chops their limbs up with a machete. I am screaming and screaming for him to stop killing, but he doesn't hear a word. Only keeps hatching away at these bodies, making their flesh fly. I pray to God please kill me now because I can't go through this again—not when the first time was enough to make me kill myself.

    I am not used to the sun setting at four in the afternoon. The days grow shorter as winter comes—shorter, colder, and harsher. It snowed on Halloween, and now, at the end of November, the weather is in a perpetual state of gray. There is nothing worse than waiting—waiting for time to pass, for the sun to set, for something to happen. I'm not going to class today. The phone rings about five times in the morning, and every time it is the same voice mail from the same people asking me where I am and what I am doing. The phone stops ringing by noon, and I am left cocooned in a pressing silence that pins me to the bed for the rest of the day.

    Maybe I should call someone. We can dress up and drink coffee and share stories over pastries. There are too many people I need to catch up with. So many lunch dates to be scheduled. I wish these things would happen, knowing that they will remain only wishes. Instead I just lay in bed for hours memorizing the cracks on the walls as the heavy gray hand presses me further down into bed. The phone stops ringing, and soon the sun disappears too and all I can do is wait for sleep. Soon it will be ten, and then it will be midnight, and then all I can wish for is a sleep without nightmares, knowing that it will not be granted.

    Earlier in ^year I signed up for a fiction-writing workshop. There is a fine line distinguishing fiction from non-fiction writing. Now that it's the end of the semester we have to present final piece. I write about a girl who has suicidal thoughts, and in telling her story, I've come up with the perfect suicide: death through submersion in a tub of concrete. While I never try it—there are no bathtubs in my dorm—I replay it so often that the thought becomes more real than life.

I can see it happening. The cashier doesn't ask any questions, though he raises his eyebrows, stares, and continues to scan bag after bag of concrete as the other man loads it onto the doll: fifteen bags of concrete and a large spade to mix it all with.

The moment I am alone in the bathroom, with my materials prepared on the floor, I rip open the first bag and then dump it into the tub. White powder flies everywhere and clings to the tips of my eyelashes. Then I open the second and dump it in after the first. Then a third, then a fourth, and the fifth, until all the bags are gone, and the bathroom is covered in white dust.

When it is all done, I strip off all my clothes and lower myself into the tub. The cold seeps to the core of me, crawling up between my legs and climbing up the rungs of my spine. It is nearly impossible to judge how long it takes to dry, for there is no clock in the room. Not even the sun changes, for the clouds cast a bleak shadow over everything beneath them. The only light that comes in through the window is gray and dismal and covers everything that it touched with a pasty glow. Time reveals itself only through the growing pain—I am being crushed and sucked apart, dehydrated and cracked in a single moment.

I try to escape by lapsing into the corpse pose again, but the pain pulls me back to the room where I lay dying, and whenever I open my eyes again, it am still be that same room, that same light, only I can't move my legs anymore or that my head can't turn or that I can't cry because my body was too dry.

My eyes search for something to focus on. There is nothing but an orange bar of soap with a few hairs on it lying on the corner of the tub. Little blue dots spread throughout the soap as well. I am counting the beads when I am overtaken by a surge of pain. My neck is bleeding. The skin along the rim of the concrete splits and cracks, and little rivulets of blood trickle down my neck and onto the surface of the concrete, where it pools into little lakes. I can see them from the corners of my eyes. The bar of soap blurs—its corners haze out, bleeding across the room until all I can see is this orange glow, shining brilliantly for one second, until it vanishes and leaves in its wake the same curtain of darkness from my nightmares.

CHAPTER 6

WHY I LIKE RIDING MY BIKE

The Milky Way as Seen from Peru (2012)
Charcoal and Chalk Pastel on Paper
24 in x 18 in

*"I want to ride my bicycle / I want to ride by bike
I want to ride by bicycle / I want to ride it where I like"*

– Queen

I LIKE TO RIDE MY BICYCLE. Sophomore year, I live in what the students call the Quad, an area on campus Harvard once used to house their women and minorities. Naturally, it is farther away from central campus than any other housing. The walk from there to the main yard takes anywhere from ten to thirty minutes, depending on how late you are or how long your legs are. It takes me thirty minutes because I am short and lazy.

After a month of skipping all my morning classes, I decide it is necessary to get a bike. I want to get a hipster bike, but the one outside of the ATA bike store near by dorm costs me nearly five hundred dollars, so I quickly go inside, down to the lower level, and ask the clerk for the least expensive bike. And there I find my prize: an olive green mountain bike with the words "DIAMOND BACK" printed in curly letters on the side. It is the smallest one and was considerably less expensive. "I'll take this one," I say, and I ride the bike home wearing my fashionable pink glasses and red flowery sundress.

There are many perks to having a bike. It's faster than walking, and it's more fun that driving. I can have the both the privileges of riding a car and being a pedestrian, and I could switch my role depending on where the traffic lay.

And, to my surprise, having a bicycle does not limit what I can wear. Through some potentially dangerous experimentation, I find out that it was possible to wear dresses and skirts while riding my bike. All I need to do is adjust the angle of my thighs and ankles, and that will stop my dress from riding up. Sometimes, if I wear a billowy dress, I ride with one hand and place the other between my legs to keep the fabric down. If I am stuck in traffic and have to maneuver a lot, I just ride standing up. I love it when I find an empty road, and I can just sit on my bike and let the inertia take me to where I need to be. All I need to do is sit and enjoy the wind, and feel good wearing my favorite dress.

My clothing choice proves to be nearly fatal on several occasions. Once, I wear a pair of boots with long laces on one of my excursions. I am riding along fine I suddenly felt a jerk when I have to pedal. I look down to see my shoelace has wrapped itself around the rod several times. I can neither pedal forward nor take my foot out, and there are cars driving on either side. Luckily, I am riding next on the right lane and can cruise my bike towards the sidewalk and untangled myself there. This happens several times: twice when I am on Mass Ave and once next to the science center.

Cars don't care if they run me over. I am going down Garden Street, towards the intersection with Mass Ave, when the car in the neighboring lane shifts into my lane. I cannot move any farther right because the side is already filled with parked cars, and I cannot stop either or the cars behind will hit me. I try to scream, but all that comes out is a small yelp. When the car is a foot away from my side I prepare to die, but then it bounces back into its lane. I am going to be okay.

In a strange sense, this danger keeps me alive. On Fridays, I will ride my bike in one direction until I get lost (which happens very easily). Sometimes it helps for me to choose one location and then make my way towards it. I ride to a nursing home in Arlington; to the medical school; to a bubble tea place in Boston; through the small neighborhoods surrounding the business school; all around the Charles.

No one knows me. All that exists is my bike and the drifting of my shadow on the road. I ride alongside with fear, and fear forces me to be fully aware of everything going on around me: of the swaying patterns of traffic, of the movements of my own body, any strange men staring at me through parked cars. I am using all of my capacities and wits to stay alive and make it back home, something that I had to do constantly when I travelled alone through South America, and that I missed doing very much. It is the adventure I crave, that somehow, in Cambridge, I can feel as free as I did when walking through Peru.

And yet, it's not about the adventure. It's not about being able to replace "walks of shame" with "rides of pride." It's not about feeling special when I furiously pedal down Mt. Auburn in a dress or racing the shuttle back from the Quad. It's the ride.

The best time to ride is at two in the morning when I make my daily trip from Pfoho, my house, to Quincy, an upperclassman house next to the Charles River. After finishing a day's worth of work, I pack up my bags, close the door, and turn off the light. The moment I hop on, I know I am done for the day, and I no longer feel trapped.

Riding away from my dorm, I see clumps of students walking towards the Quad—some are probably marching to their late night love nest, others from a late meeting with Lamont. I pedal down Garden Street, and I am the only person who exists in the world. Cambridge becomes an entirely different city late on a Monday night. Not even a single car drives by, and I smile knowing that I am the best friend I have at that moment. I am stirred by my sudden lack of thought, and it turns into a smile.

Sometimes I sing, sometimes I don't. Sometimes I wear my leather gloves, sometimes I forget to.

Silence does move, and it moves inside of me. The current of my mind adjusts to the topography of the landscape, and for once in the day, I am at peace. Once I reach Harvard Square I ride past CVS and see two homeless men smoking, and I think of Mickey, who I met at the homeless shelter a year ago, and wonder if he is still alive. Strangers surround me, and yet I feel at home. I see a man walking alone on the street and wonder if he is sharing my serenity. Perhaps he knows what I'm up to. I don't mind, because I know my secrets will be guarded in the stillness of the night. There is an unwritten code of silence, and all of us stragglers understand that.

This is why I ride my bike. I live for these moments of transition, these moments of change, for it is being between two points that I am forced to live in the present. I avoid the shuttle at all costs because I don't want my moments of transition to be ruined by the constant talk and interjection of people in my head. Whenever I talk to people, I am letting them enter me momentarily. If I do not take time to realign myself, I will be cut to pieces. This needs to be time set aside every day to heal.

And so, for seven and a half minutes every day, starting at around two in the morning, I take my bike out and begin my meditation. I ride in this blissful solitude for seven and a half precious minutes, observing the world through the eyes of an infant until I reach the gates of Quincy. Every night, I finish this journey knowing that something had just happened, something beautiful and too subtle to be put into words.

I park my bike and I take off my gloves, if I am wearing them, and then move forward again.

CHAPTER 7

MY CACTUS EARL

Soft Still Life with Tutu and Snake (2012)
Graphite on Paper
16 in x 20 in

"My baby don't care for shows / My baby don't care for clothes / My baby just cares for me."

— Nina Simone

I HAVE A PET CACTUS, and his name is Earl. The truth is: I love Earl. In fact, I get along with him better than I do with the majority of people. Unlike humans, Earl doesn't talk back or expect anything from me. He just sits on my windowsill and takes in whatever sunlight New England has to offer. He doesn't bother making trouble with the other objects on the windowsill. He's happy with just being himself—a tiny, green, three-and-a-half-inch-long, photosynthesizing, spiny dick-shaped thing sticking out of the ground.

I've had Earl for a little over a month now. That's about three percent of his life (Earl is three years old). I received him as a sort of "Sisterhood of the Traveling Pants" gift. My two best friends and I had known each other since the eighth grade. Unfortunately college placed some distance between us, as I was the only one who left Georgia. Right before sophomore year, the three of us met up again in my friend's room. I noticed a cactus sitting on her desk, picked it up, and couldn't resist cooing at it. "You should keep him," she said, smiling.

So I did.

I was a bit nervous going to the airport. I was really afraid that they wouldn't let him through because I know they usually don't allow pets or plants on any international flight. But I figured—this is a domestic flight, and Earl wouldn't hurt anybody ... his spines are fuzzy. But just in case something happened, I asked my parents to stand outside of the security line so that I could give them Earl if he couldn't pass. They wait.

I walked up to the security line and handed my ID to the man at the counter. He saw Earl in my hand, looked at me, and said, "You'd better not eat that thing—I hear they're poisonous." He smiled and let me through.

The real panic came at the security line. I didn't think I could carry Earl in my hands through the scan. I couldn't put him on the conveyer belt either because a million monstrosities could happen to him—he could get knocked off, he could get confiscated, he could get tipped over or caught in one of the grooves and lose all his soil. Luckily, I figure out that I could nestle him inside one of the trays.

I went through the scan and looked back in anticipation at the man overlooking the scans. A few beats passed, and I knew that Earl was safe when the man turned back, gave me a weird look and shook his head. He was trying hard not to smile.

I pranced to my gate, with cactus in one hand and luggage in the other, smiling like a fool who just got laid.

Not only did does Earl behave extraordinarily well, but he has also made me a lot of friends. During the plane ride, I put Earl on the seat next to me while I was getting my things in order. Suddenly, I felt a shadow, and I looked up to see a 27-year-old guy standing over me. "Uh ... Why is there a cactus in my seat?"

We ended up talking for the whole plane ride.

Sometimes I take Earl on walks. The first thing I do when I get back on campus my sophomore year is put on my best white cotton dress, fashionable pink sunglasses, gladiator shoes, and strut around school with my cactus. I make sure to cover lots of ground so that I can give him the full range of Harvard soil. Poor Earl barely had his roots covered when I first got him.

Sometimes I really worry about Earl. If a window is left open, he can get cold and shrivel. If there isn't enough sun, he might get depressed and shed off his spines and die. One day, I take him on a walk and bring him to my boyfriend's dorm on the other side of campus (Perhaps giving Earl a father figure would inspire him to grow). I leave Earl there overnight and am too busy for the next few days to bring him back to my place. On the third day, William puts Earl on the balcony outside his window so that he can get some full sunshine. When I come to his dorm and ask where Earl was, he points towards the window, and I see my little cactus nearly toppling over the ledge as a breeze comes through. I scream and run to save Earl's life.

That same day I snuggle Earl into my basket beside some textbooks and a jacket and bike him all the way back to my dorm, which is a mile away. Earl nearly falls out several times, and he loses about half of his soil by the end of the trip.

I still take Earl on additional walks (he now has full soil again). When he's at home he sits on my windowsill overlooking the Quad yard. Sometimes he has company—my neighbor has an aloe plant named Aloe, and for a while the two became companions—but mostly, Earl sits by himself on the windowsill.

After closely examining Earl so many times, I have decided that Cacti are fascinating plants. Earl, in particular, is a column-shaped cactus. His whole body is divided into ribs. These things are called tubercles, and each tubercle is covered in little white cushions called areoles, which have spines protruding out of them. Spines can either be very thick, dense or fuzzy and light-colored. Earl has the latter. They're more like thick hairs than spines, and they stick out in jumbled directions over his body.

Earl has a tuft of hair at the top, which I pet a lot. This section, which I call the head, is also greener than the rest of his shaft.

This part of Earl's anatomy has puzzled me for a very long time. But I look at him closely again one day, and suddenly notice that Earl grew an extra areole on each of his tubercles. All of a sudden, Earl has grown four millimeters! Apparently, the top of the cactus contains many parenchymal cells, which have thin cell walls and are capable of frequent division. These allow the plant to grow. This is what Earl spends all his time on: he sits staring at the sun all day, gathering and photosynthesizing and collecting enough little molecules until he has enough to produce an extra areole. He secretes the new forms out of the tip of his head, and they gradually move down his body, like a beautiful, life-giving, slow motion ejaculation.

Cacti make especially good pets because they thrive off of negligence, which I provide a lot of. It can be very comforting to know that I can come back, regardless of what I've done or who I've become, and still have the same cactus waiting for me. To be honest, Earl never really changes because he doesn't grow that much. I've long since given up on trying to make him become a macho cactus. Instead, I just try to keep him from dying. So I set him next to my sun box. It's supposed to be for me, to keep me happy when there is no sun, but I have found that keeping Earl alive is enough to keep me happy. In the end, we're both just trying to stay alive.

CHAPTER 8

OAKWOOD LODGE

Hell is Other People (2012)
Acrylic and Chalk Pastel on Cardboard
20 in x 16 in

"And how do you know that you're mad? 'To begin with,' said the Cat, 'a dog's not mad. You grant that?' I suppose so, said Alice. 'Well then,' the Cat went on, 'you see a dog growls when it's angry, and wags it's tale when it's pleased. Now I growl when I'm pleased, and wag my tail when I'm angry. Therefore I'm mad.'"

– Lewis Caroll, *Alice's Adventures in Wonderland*

"Let's go crazy, let's get nuts / Look for the purple banana / 'Til they put us in the truck, let's go."

– Prince

FIRST CLASS

TWO PARAMEDICS PICK ME up from the University Health Center, perhaps expecting me to be crying, pulling out my hair or sitting limp in a chair. What they get instead is a terrifyingly normal looking girl who smiles a lot. I feel like a queen when they put me on top of the stretcher. I had been in the waiting room of the university health center for hours now, and being wheeled away from the dingy waiting room feels like being escorted first class away from limbo.

I haven't been in such a good mood in a long time. Inside the ambulance, as the paramedic takes my blood pressure and heart rate. She looks young, only a few years older than me.

"Where did you go to school?" I ask.

"Me?" she says. "Well, I graduated from BU a couple of years ago." She reaches over me to reach for the thermometer, and I notice something interesting about her ring.

"Where'd you get that ring?" I ask. "It's pretty awesome."

"Oh, this thing." She lifts up her finger, "There's an old man who comes on campus a lot to sell things, and one day I got this from him." She lets me take a closer look. On top of the ring, two people have sex missionary style.

"Ooh, is, is are they doing what I think they're doing?"

"Yep," she says, grinning a bit. "It is indeed."

When we arrive at the hospital, they wheel me into a small, square room with two doors and a large window facing the nursing station. The driver, a young man also looks like a recent college graduate, grows very concerned for me as we enter the room. I am still tied down to the stretcher and am holding my backpack in my lap. Suddenly, I hear a small splintering sound beneath me. I look down—it is a pair of the split-apart wooden chopsticks. I got them from a Chinese restaurant the night before and slipped them into the front pocket of my backpack.

The young man gasps and hunches over to grab the chopsticks. He looks ashamed of himself. He wipes them off on his shirt and hands them to me. "H-here you go ma'am—I'm so sorry they dropped," he says, and steps back with his head hung and his hands folded behind his back.

"Oh, thank you!" I say, smiling, and place them back in my backpack. I want to reassure him that I will still be able to eat even if I don't have chopsticks, and that a small disturbance like that will not make me breakdown and start attacking people.

Nurses file in and out of my room. Soon there are stacks of paperwork, needles in my arm, and a doctor wearing purple scrubs. At last, when midnight arrives, I am alone. "Whatever happens now can only be good," I tell myself. I change into my pajamas in the bathroom around the corner, turn the lights off and sink into a deep sleep.

The murmurs come in the middle of the night: shadows moving around my room. From the few words I can discern, I know that a bed is available somewhere, and we are leaving now. The door from the nurse's side opens, and in come three men. "Let's go," they say.

This time there is no stretcher. The men are tired and focused just on getting the job done. They look at all my bags, filled with clothes and books, which my friends had brought me and give me an incredulous look. Still, one of the men takes my bags for me, and I follow behind carrying only my backpack. I want to put on a bra, but feel too shy to ask. I figure the dark will hide my body from them.

The ambulance ride is quiet. I sit on the bench beside my paramedic, who is also lost in thought. Behind me, the highway stretches on and disappears into the dark horizon. Only a few other cars are out on the road with us. It is four thirty in the morning, and we are still far from our destination. I take a look at the man next to me. I wonder how many kids had sat in this very spot, and what they had acted like.

"What's your name?" I ask.

He looks up, and I can't tell if he's smiling or not in the dark. "Alex," he says. "And yours?"

"My Ngoc. Like 'Me knock on door." I hear him chuckle.

"So, uh, what school you go to?"

"Harvard," I say.

"Ooo-weee. It must be hard there."

"Yeah."

"Was school really stressful or something?"

"Yeah," I say, knowing that it is much more complicated than that. "Its just overwhelming, and I want to get myself away from everything, you know?"

"Yeah, that ain't a bad idea." We ask each other a few more questions until a silence settles in the conversation. I change the topic and said, "Do you know much about this place?"

"Yep," he sighs. "Been up here a couple of times. Seems like a decent enough place. I've heard some things about it though."

I grunt in response.

Then he bends in closer and says, "Look here. I know you're a smart girl. Don't be worried. When you get there, just say what they want you to say, work with your doctors, and you should be out in a couple of days."

I thank him for his advice, and we continue talking for a while until the ambulance slows down. We are pulling up into a gravel driveway. When the car finally stops, Alex jumps out, and moments later, the back door opens, revealing a gray, silent night outside. The hospital looks more like a country house because of its outer wood paneling. It is only one story tall. We walk to entrance, and inside, Alex and the driver exchange some paperwork with someone behind the door. Before leaving, he turns to me and says, "Hey, it was good meeting you. Remember what I said, mmmk?" He shakes my hand. "Good luck."

Inside, I meet the night nurse, an old, black lady whose body sags on her bones. We go down a narrow hallway lined with doors on either side. Each one has a small square window near the top. The hallway opens into a common room with plastic blue chairs arranged in a square. A cleaning lady is spraying each one with a bottle of Lysol. In the corner is a water cooler, and at the other end of the room a hallway that leads to somewhere I cannot see.

"Here honey, let me take your bags." The nurse speaks with a strange accent. She takes out some keys and opens a door--a bathroom. "Oonduress."

"What?"

"Oonduress," she says.

"What?"

She hands me a hospital gown, and then I understand. "Oh, give me your shoes too." She closes the door, and I can hear her footsteps fading away outside.

Minutes later, she comes back. My navy blue blazer, which has metal buttons, is gone. My boots have no shoelaces on them. In place of my bags is a single paper bag containing a fraction of my clothes. My laptop and cellphone are both nowhere in sight.

After I put my clothes back on, she shows me next door to a larger room with two sagging couches, some stacked blue chairs, and a table against the far wall. A young girl comes in and does the paperwork with me. I place my signature on page after page, not really paying attention to what she is saying. She is too cheery against the fluorescent lights.

She leaves, and shortly afterwards the psychiatrist comes in. He sits on the couch directly in front of me and introduces himself. I don't catch his name though—I am too busy studying him. He looks Hispanic, and rather refined. Though he is tired, his eyes are still alert, and the stubble on his face is fringed with bits of gray hair. He looks like Ricardo Darin, the famous Argentinian actor.

"Are you in college?" asks Dr. Ricardo.

"Yes," I say.

"What school do you go to?"

"Um, Harvard."

"Ah, yes," he says. "I used to teach there." He looks nostalgic for a second, with his eyes averted, and then snaps back into focus. "So, um, My Ngoc," can you tell me a little bit of what was going on?"

I forget how many times I have already recounted this story in the past two days, but I tell him again, trying to make it sound as genuine as possible. "I was suicidal," I say. "I was in my room and wanted to cut myself with a knife."

It was the knife my dad had packed especially for me. "Here, you can use this to cut up vegetables to eat with your ramen late at night," he said as he carefully wrapped the blade up with layers of newspaper.

"Yeah," I tell Dr. Ricardo. "It was scary, so I wasn't sure if I would be safe if I went back to my room, so I chose to be hospitalized."

He nods his head. "What were your symptoms like in the weeks before?"

I tell him about all those mornings where I lay in bed for hours, the nightmares I had and the crying fits that came almost every night. "Towards the end," I say, "I was afraid of people. Like, when I was in my room and wanted to go the bathroom, if I opened the door and heard footsteps in the hallway, I would immediately close the door and wait until the hallway was quiet before leaving."

After taking a few notes, he asks me if I'm okay with taking a light antidepressant. "Lexapro. It's a new drug, and a lot of people have had success with it."

I remain silent for a while. The last person who asked me that was the school nurse, earlier in the spring. After listening to my story for about five minutes, she asked, "So, do you want to take medicine?" Just before going to that appointment, I had watched Prozac Nation, so of course, I declined, wondering how such a big decision could just be left up to the patient. And besides, I was sure I had nothing so serious as to require medicine. I left with only a light box.

Eight months later, I am having this same conversation again. This time I nod, "Yeah, medicine sounds good." He leaves, and I am finally free to go to my bedroom.

In the middle of the night I wake up to get some water. Back down the hallway. There are a few people up. Something large buzzes past me. It takes me a few seconds to grasp that it is a fat kid pretending to be an airplane. Farther down the hall, two people sit in the plastic blue chairs: a young teenager with a small head and squeaky voice and an older man speaking in low tones. I grab my water, nod at them and retreat to my bed.

The pillows are not very fluffy, and the mattress is hard, but for the first time in a long time, I can sleep without nightmares.

MAKING THE BED

Someone is screaming. At least, I think it is screaming. I listen more closely. No, no one is screaming, just people talking very loudly. There are some odd clanking noises accompanying the voices. A high-pitched girl's voice. A deeper, heavier chorus of men's voices. It is not a comforting arrangement of sounds though, like those which my parents make early in the morning before they go to work: the hum of mom's voice floating over the sound of pots and pans clinking in the sink; the hum of the garage; the sturdy thuds of my dad's footsteps descending the stairs. No. There is something wrong with what I'm hearing. I lay in bed as still as I can, like a stunned rabbit, listening for any sounds of predators nearby. The voices belong to young people, but the sound is off. I think of the boy I saw last night. The people making these noises are not normal.

I can't tell what objects were making the noises. It sounds like someone is slapping someone, or someone is slamming large objects on a table. The energy is uncontrolled—there is no rhythm to the sounds, like the motions of a robot going berserk.

Eventually I drift back to sleep. Occasionally I wake up, convinced that people are opening my door and looking at me. But every time, I look up and only see an empty room. I rest my head against the pillow, taking in as much comfort as possible.

"My Ngoc?" A voice. Older this time. Normal. I look up to see two women standing at my bedside. "Hi, my name is Dr. Mango, and this is Kayla. She will be your social worker. How are you doing this morning?"

I mumble something in response.

"Very well," Dr. Mango says. She goes on to explain some other things, and then they both leave. I wonder why I need a social worker but fall asleep before I can think of any answer.

Not long after, another voice calls, "My Ngoc?"

I open my eyes again. This time the sound is closer to the door. I don't have my contact lenses on, so she remains a blurry figure in the distance. "Do you want to go to group session? It's starting in ten minutes."

What is group session? "Do I have to go?" I ask.

"No, it's okay," she says, and leaves. I stay in bed a bit longer, trying my best to dissect the noises coming from all round me. By now I am sure that my door was being opened and closed. I even see someone's head poking into my room at one point.

"My Ngoc?" Another fuzzy shape at the door. A woman's voice asks me if I want to go to group. Again, she says it's not necessary, but I remember what the ambulance driver said, and tell her I will be going right away.

I get out of my bed, strip off my pajamas and change into day clothes, taking a pair of jeans and a light pink sweater from the bookshelf. I usually leave my clothes on the floor, but something tells me I need to be as neat as possible. Anything that doesn't please the nurses will go against me in the future, so I pick my clothes up and fold them carefully into the bookshelf.

I am about to go when I notice how sloppy my bed looks. I think of what my mom would say if she were here. "You are so sloppy! You can't even make your bed right! The sheets are still crooked and you just threw the pillows on!" Sometimes, she would even rearrange my sheets for me, shaking her head the whole time. "I'm such a horrible mom. I can never teach my kids anything." Then she would turn to me and say, "You absolutely need to make your bed, you hear? If you can't even make your bed how will you ever accomplish anything else?"

I fluff up my one pillow and place it neatly at the center of the bed. I take off the comforter, smooth out the starch white sheets, chosen to show even the slightest drops of blood and human excretions, and tuck their ends under the mattress. Afterwards I lay the comforter on top, making sure that there is not a single wrinkle at the top. I inspect my work.

My mom would have been proud.

Wondering what in the world "group" is, I leave my room and walk down the hallway towards the common room. The chairs are now filled with people—mostly teenagers slouched at all different sorts of angles. I don't have time to put on my contacts, so I squint for an empty seat. There is one in the far corner between a young girl with matted hair and a younger black boy who is looking down at the floor. Several people around the room nod slightly, acknowledging my entrance into the congregation. I had come in while they were introducing names. "Hello my name is Scott," pipes up a chubby boy in the corner. He has a lot of fat collecting in all the wrong places, making his face look odd and swollen. Then, a sullen boy to the right mutters his name. We are moving clockwise. Occasionally, an elder man or woman will stalk, and a wave of relief washes over me as I hear the familiar speech patterns. My heart picks up its pace again when I see that these people have nametags. When they finish going around the circle, it's my turn.

I speak, trying to seem as friendly as possible. I don't want to make any enemies this early on.

"Well, then," says one of the women with the nametags. "Tom, would you like to read the community rules for us?" It takes her a long time to say it—she pronounces each word with utmost care.

A boy across from me reaches for a crinkled sheet of paper on his lap. While most speakers will hold the paper somewhere away from their face, he holds his directly in front of him, and it is hard to hear anything he says. He, however, is unaware of this effect. He puts the list down when he finishes stuttering through the list. We're all proud of his accomplishment. "Thank you, Tom," the woman says.

Why does this place need community rules? Why is it necessary to sit in a circle like this? Everyone else around the room is unfazed. The men and women seem mostly tired, and the teens impatient. Just as I am getting used to being in the circle, it breaks apart. The grownups stand up, stretch, and then file to the front of the room. The teens remain in their seats and wait.

"Okay guys, it's time to fill in your goal sheets," says a man. When he speaks, all the kids looked up at him. Some moan and grunt, but they all oblige themselves to line up and take a sheet. I, too, follow.

There are little black grains all over the paper—evidence of having been photocopied over and over again. The questions stare up at me: What are your goals for today? What improvements have you made? What is your goal for the week?

Find out where I am. Glad I am in safe place. Get even better. I scrawl my responses on the page. There is another handout, but before I get to it, a shadow comes across my page. I look up to see a large face looming above me.

It's one of the biggest kids in the group. It looks like baby fat has collected in copious amounts all over his body, making his limbs look like rubber. He stands a foot in front of me, unaware that he is too close. "Hey there, I'm Max." His eyes bulge. "You know, when you first walked in, everyone thought you were the cutest girl in the room." I think I saw him smacking his lips. "You know, me and my girlfriend, we be havin a lotta trouble lately." He flexes his other arm.

So the kids stay here long enough to date each other. I glance sideways at the adults, who are just looking on apathetically. "Oh, I'm sorry to hear that," I tell him.

"Yeah, it's been rough." He spreads his legs, and his crotch is at my face. I keep my gaze directed upwards. "But, you know, I'm thinking of breaking up with her soon."

"Oh? I'm sorry to hear. What's her name?" I ask. A string of words come out of his mouth, but I have a hard time listening. My vision blurs. One of the adults finally calls on him to turn in his worksheets.

Once he leaves, I fill out the second page. It first tells me that it is important to have a good sense of humor and then asks me to write down some jokes. I hand everything in, along with the blunt pencil they gave me, to the man in charge and run back to my room.

I scramble to find the paperwork they handed me last night. I have stacked them neatly in a pile in the corner of the bottom right shelf. Now, I pour through them, looking for any clue words that could ground me. Like the worksheets, these pages also have evidence of being photocopied many times before. I wonder why they didn't just update the forms.

Something about voluntary admission—I had come here by consent. Do some people actually go here against their will? Another line about hiring a lawyer if I feel like I am being detained for no reason. Detained? These are both universal forms that are required by the state of Massachusetts. I flip through more papers and find that I'm looking for: a packet of rules and regulations. I look mostly for the bolded words that indicated headings. Visitors: I can see guests in a private place. Conduct. I always behave well, so I move past that section until I see called "Patient's Rights." I pick out only a few keywords, my mind too frantic to be able to string them into sentences. "Psychiatric" in one sentence and then "locked doors" in another.

And then it hits me: I am in the loony bin.

BROKEN TOE

I need to tell someone that I'm here. Frantic, I step out of my room and walk towards the nurse's desk. "Um, what is the name of this place?"

They look at me like I'm crazy. "It's Oakwood, honey."

"Um, can I please use the phone?"

"You have to use the one in the hallway, sweetie."

I look over. Angie is on the phone. "Um, Angie's on the phone," I say. "Can I please use this phone?"

The man behind the desk sighs and hands me a slip of paper. I scribble down the number to my dad's nail salon and hand it back to him. He dials it and hands the receiver to me.

I hear it ringing, ringing, ringing, and it just keeps on ringing. It dawns on me that my parents don't have voicemail set up on the nail stores phones, so it will keep on ringing until the person calling gives up all hope. I give up all hope and hand the phone back to the man. "They didn't answer," I say. "Can I please dial another number?"

The paper comes back my way.

Now I write down the number to my mom's salon. The paper goes back to him, then the receiver to me. Ring, ring, ring, ad infinitum. No one picks up. "Please, can I try one more?" I ask. He's getting impatient, but he still gives me the paper again. This time I try my dad's cell phone. It goes straight to his voicemail.

"Um, sir?"

"Yeah?" he growls.

"No one is picking up... I just called my dad but... can I try again?" I call home, I call my mom's cell phone, I call my sister's phone. No one picks up, and every time I hand the receiver back to the nurse, I can tell he pities me. I can't take it anymore—I have to go back to my room. The shame of loneliness follows me through the hallway, and I feel like I am wearing a badge that marks me "lost" for all others to see. I cry myself to the point of exhaustion, and then it becomes obvious that there will be no end to this if I just keep on crying.

I resolve to make another phone call—this time to William. He is the only other person whose phone number I have memorized. The phone is still being used though, so I stand in the hallway waiting. Max walks by and sees me standing alone.

"Oh man, you look like you need a hug," he says. My instant urge is to run over and press my face against his enormous belly. So far, he's been the first person here to show me sympathy. But I restrain myself and instead hug him from the side.

The nurses see us hugging and shout for us to stop. I wonder what is wrong. Later on I learn that patients are never allowed to touch each other. In my case, touch has little consequences because I am cognitively intact, but it's not always this way. Sometime nurses will walk into the kitchen to find one patient giving another oral sex and then have to break them apart.

The phone is soon free. I dial William's number, and he picks up on the second ring.

A few hours later, while I am in bed, a nurse knocks gently on my door. "My Ngoc, you have a visitor."

It's him. The nurses won't let me see him in my room, even though we showed them the papers that said we could be seen in private. All around us, the kids are staring with their eyebrows furrowed. Slanted, angry eyes follow our every action. People here don't get visitors very often.

"Ummm, I got you some cupcakes," he says. "But the nurses took them away—"

Suddenly a screeching sound erupts from the corner.

Angie is strangling the boy sitting next to her. Her eyes are squinted, with tears trickling out of the corners. She grimaces and screams things I do not understand. The other boy can only let out tiny gasps. The commotion does not last long, for the nurses move quickly, but it is long enough for me to see that the entire time, Angie is not looking at Eddie, but straight at me.

With everything quiet again, other than the occasional sound of Angie sniffling in the corner, William and I try to resume our conversation. We don't hold hands, because any sign of affection might make the others crack again.

"So, uh, how are your classes going? I'm sorry for all this William. I don't want you to be stressed."

He stops talking to me, and simply holds my gaze. I can tell that a million thoughts and questions and plans are bursting around behind his eyes.

Suddenly, boom.

Another boom. And then —

BOOM.

William and I jerk up from our seats. The fat airplane kid from last night has risen from his chair and is moving towards the front of the room, kicking the walls with his enormous feet as he goes. Boom. Every hit makes the entire building shake, and the sounds of his rage echo against the bare walls and the cold, peeling linoleum floor. Once he reaches the nurse's desk, he rams the walls with his hands, making a sharper, more painful sound. I can see the wall vibrating.

"Hey there, big boy." It's the headman. He goes on very gently. "What's going on?" Again, he doesn't seem to care about this show. I watch them talk. The boy has stopped ramming the walls and is now growling. That, too, stops, and he resorts to standing on one foot and leaning against the wall, listening to the headman talk.

"Did you see that?" William asks.

"See what?"

"Him," he says, craning his head towards the boy. "He broke his toe."

"What? How do you know?"

"When he kicked his foot against the wall he winced but the nurses didn't see. Look, he's bending over now."

William leaves soon after that. "Don't worry, My Ngoc. I'm going to get you out of here." He squeezes my hand and goes down the hallway. William doesn't know yet, but there are now only three cupcakes in that box instead of four because while we had been sitting, one of the nurses had come by and eaten one.

I stay in my room for the rest of day. I come out once in the evening to get dinner and attend the second group session. Having calmed down, I decide to talk to one of the kids sitting alone in the middle of the room. He looks about fourteen. His parents must have been attractive; he has good features, but his eyes are downcast and lonely. I set my tray next to him. "Can I sit with you?"

He looks up and scoots over. "What's your name?" I ask.

"Tyrone," he says, still pushing his macaroni and cheese around with his plastic fork.

"That's cool. My name is My Ngoc."

He nods.

We have lunches similar to those I had in elementary school. "Where are you from?"

"Maryland," he says. "Where you from?"

"I'm from Atlanta."

"Oh I have a brother there."

"Do you have any other brothers or sisters?"

"Well, I had lotsa brothers and sisters everywhere. Got one in St. Louis I think. And some more in California. My dad was a pimp, and he traveled a lot, you know."

"Ah, I see." I say, not sure how else to respond. We eat some more, and I think of another question to ask. "How did you get here?"

"My friend, he robbed my house, but then my mom thought I did it, so I went to jail, and then they put me here, and I been going around from here to foster family and then back here."

Max walks across the room, towards the bathroom, like a whale undulating its way through a school of fish. Another kid, Gary sits on some chairs across from us and stares straight at me.

"Do you know how Gary got in? He's always smiling. He seems too nice to do anything."

"Oh, that guy?" Terry points. I nod. "He followed a girl home."

"Ah." I poke my straw through the orange juice cup. "Do you have any friends here?"

He shakes his head. I think I am the first person here who talks to him like a friend. I can't see anything wrong with him. He just seems unwanted, and these are the only places that will take him. I grab some extra napkins, ask for some pencils and play a drawing game with him.

Ten o' clock is bedtime. After showering and brushing my teeth, I retire to my room, ready to rest. It is hard to fall asleep though. The sounds from outside keep on coming in, just as they did in the morning. I hear Angie's voice again. She's only two bedrooms down from me. "I don't want to be he-e-e-e-ere!" She moans. "I don't want to be he-e-e-e-e-ere!" Occasionally, a shout or two explodes in the distance, like accent notes harmonizing to the main line of Angie's wailing.

There is even a percussion part. Next door to me is a room with a single punching bag. Max is in there, and he provides the guiding rhythm for the song, a beat, which is as idiosyncratic and restless as the rest of the symphony. "Get me out of here!" Angie shouts. BOOM. The house vibrates. "Why am I so sa-a-a-ad?" BOOM. BOOM. I feel like the ceiling is about to break. A squeal here, two shouts from the tenors. "I don't be lo-o-ong here!" Boom. I can feel their hearts wrenching.

Where do these kids come from? I want so bad to hold them, but I am afraid that they will hurt me. Listening to their song, I know I am not any different from them. We all understand too well the language of pain, and while they wear theirs on their sleeves, I bury mine inside. Yet, regardless of where we keep it, none of us know how to channel our pain, and it ends up welling inside of us until it transforms into something else, something with a heavier form and more evil intentions. That something had nearly killed me, and today, it snapped a toe in half.

CHAPTER 9

BEHIND THE CURTAIN

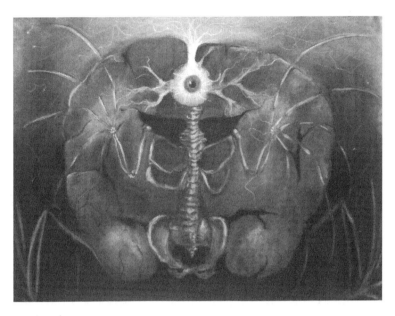

Mediation (2012)
Charcoal and Graphite on Paper
26 in x 18 in

"Each friend represents a world in us, a world not born until they arrive, and it is only by this meeting that a new world is born."

—Anais Nin

"Our whole life is solving puzzles."

—Erno Rubik

I HAVE NOT TOUCHED a puzzle in eleven years. Now, here I am, perched on a red and white loveseat sorting my way through a five hundred piece jig-saw of a beach scene: a wooden boat beneath two palm trees. It is 9:30 in the morning. I had just met with my team, which consisted of Laila, a social worker, and Dr. White-Bateman, a young, thin doctor who wore fancy silk blouses and pronounced every word with utmost care in her tiny, raspy voice. They went through their list of questions. How have you slept? How is your appetite? Do you hear any voices or have racing thoughts in your head? And, of course, the Biggie: Have you had any thoughts of hurting yourself or others recently?

Have I been thinking of suicide lately?

Of course not. I have a puzzle to do.

I run my hand over my cheeks. They are a bit dry, but smoother than ever. Everything here at McLean is clean. The ventilation system sucks everything out of the air, including the moisture.

This is a safe place, I think to myself. The short-term inpatient care unit has four wings that branch from the central nurse station, each with its own lounge. There is a kitchen, a common area with a TV, a puzzle station, and even an upright piano on one of the wings. So far no patients have strangled each other. Rather, they speak softly and move like gentle fish through the hallways. I can use the bathroom without having to ask for permission, and I can even have my own pencils. McLean is the best psychiatric hospital in the nation. I've only been at McLean for a day, but it already feels like heaven.

On the second day of my stay at Oakwood, one of the nurses called me over and told me that I could gather my belongings. Apparently, many phone calls had been made between the University Health Services, my resident dean and the God knows what other bureaucracies when they found out I was sent to Oakwood. Usually Harvard students go directly to McLean or a hospital in the Cambridge area. Whatever exchanges had been made, they were successful in getting me out of there. On that same day, a new girl arrived to the ward. She was very bright, pretty, and alarmingly normal. However, I could tell that there was a knot deep inside her. She looked scared and on guard. I asked her if I could draw a picture of her. As I'm sketching, I tell her, "You're a smart girl. Just follow the rules and do what you think the nurses want, and you should be out of here in no time."

After that I packed my bags and said goodbye to Tyrone, to Max, to Angie, and all the others that I had gotten to know in the past thirty-six hours. This time I knew not to give them any hugs. Angie shouted, "You're leaving already? Please, take me with you please!" Where did these kids come from, and where were they going to go after this? One girl was going to go back to community college, but most of them had no foreseeable future other. Most would remain at Oakwood until the government stopped wanting to pay for them, at which they would then go in and out of foster care until they reached eighteen years of age. After that, homelessness would be just around the corner.

When I stepped through the door, unlocked just for me to step outside, I felt like a prisoner released. In just two days the leaves had taken on a new coat of colors, and a breeze was blowing the red and yellow leaves around my ankles. I thought of all the kids still sitting in the common and felt a rush of guilt for not being able to take them all with me to the best psychiatric hospital in the nation. All of a sudden the beauty of autumn turned bittersweet.

No one knows why I was sent to Oakwood. It was a bug in the computer system, a mistake by the administration. I believe that everything happens for a reason though, and my trip to Oakwood was meant for me to meet all the people that I met.

I flip over some more of the pieces. This is my least favorite part. Whenever I pour out the puzzles contents I want to fit them together immediately. I force myself to turn them all over before I move on. Soon, I have the border finished. I work on the sand at the bottom – the light pieces are easiest to spot. From there I work my way up, watching the picture slowly form itself.

On the first morning, I ask a nurse if I can use my makeup. He walks with me to get my leopard makeup bag from the closet, and we walk together to the restroom. While he waits outside, I stand in front of the mirror, with the door open behind me, and rummage around my bag. The little bottles clink against each other, loud against the silence of the hospital. I skip some of my usual routine—I do not put on liquid black eyeliner because it takes too much time, and I do not put on as much eye shadow because I do not want to keep the nurse waiting too long. I step out of the restroom, my face freshly covered in powder and my eyes smothered with purple eye shadow. I shyly hand over the bag and scurry away.

The next morning, I ask for my make-up again, only this time, the nurse doesn't have to accompany me. One successful night in the hospital had raised my privileges up. They erased the "s" next to my name on the whiteboard in front of the nurse's station this morning, so now I can use sharps without supervision. I walk down the same corridor towards the same bathroom. On my way I pass a patient talking to his nurse. They speak in low tones, seated across from each other. "How are you feeling today, Tom?"

He stares at her with the look of the dead. "Good."

"Have you been sleeping okay?"

The same blankness. His muscles don't seem to attach together correctly. "Yes."

"Have you been having any thoughts of hurting yourself?"

A pause. "Yes," quieter than ever.

I feel bad for listening and slipped into the bathroom. I repeat the same procedure. Dab on the nose. Dab on the cheek. I am about to put on my eyeliner when I pause and stare at my reflection in the mirror. It looks like I have just wrapped a dead person's skin on my face. I decide that it's silly to wear foundation in a psych ward, wash off all filth from my face and then store my makeup bad away for good. When I leave the bathroom, the room is empty except for ghost of their conversation.

I have some new friends. Five kids about my age: Sarah, a pretty young blond who has panic attacks; Neil, a cheery, chubby high school drop-out who was temporarily homeless, and is now taking courses at the Courdon Bleu to be- come a chef; Tess, a BU student who voluntarily came to readjust her medications, which had suddenly stopped working; Nick, a Tufts senior who woke up one morning and swallowed too many pills; and James, a college student who drove his car eighty miles an hour into a tree and emerged from the accident without a single scratch.

We find ourselves idling in the kitchen at around 8:30 in the evening. Someone wants to play a game.

Breaking the hesitation, I suggest hide and seek.

Ten minutes later, I am hiding behind a curtain, giggling. The last time I played hide and seek was on a farm in Argentina. And before that when we still lived in the old apartment complex. Ever since I sensed that my childhood lacked attention, I made up for the years of solitude the best I could in random places, even if it had to be a psych ward.

Almost two minutes have passed by when my nurse comes through the door at my side. She shrieks when she sees me hiding behind the curtain.

"My Ngoc! What are you doing?" she screams.

My answer doesn't satisfy her.

The game quickly breaks up as we track down all the participants. The five of us collect in the hallway as the nurses tell us in strict, maternal voices that we cannot play hide and seek because the staff will not be able to find us for the fifteen-minute checks. We hang our heads low, but we are all smiling, eyes, mouths and all.

On Friday, almost a week since I first got to McLean, I get a phone call from Chi Ti. My heart melts when I hear my Chi Nhung's voice in the background. They're here to visit. They arrive with bags and bags of Thai food. When we finish eating, Chi Nhung asks if she can pray for me. We go to my room because someone started shouting in the dining room just when we were about to pray. We gather on the bed, hold hands and lower our heads. She begins her prayer:

"Jesus, I come to you today to please forgive me for being such a bad sister. I'm so sorry for not paying more attention to Buoi when this was happening to her. Please, God, protect my sister and give her your strength and help her heal during these times. Because..." She pauses, like she's choking—I hear a sniffle. "Because I know and you know that humans are so limited, and we can't... we can't and... we are so weak. Sometimes we can't handle it all Lord." Chi Ti is crying, and when I hear her cry, a feeling overtakes me, and I cry too. Chi Nhung continues, "Thank you for allowing me to be here with my little sister right now, for the three of us to share this prayer with you. Please love her when I cannot, please—I pray the best for Buoi. I pray in the name of Jesus Christ..."

"Amen," we all say. When the prayer is over, we all look up and around at each other, at the red rimmed eyes and trembling mouths curved into faint smiles, and we know that something special just happened.

Chi Nhung stands up and puts her hand on my head. She had not flown in almost a decade but left her three young children behind to visit me here. I hug her, placing my head on her stomach. She feels so warm. When I look up, I see her smiling down at me with gentlest expression. There is something about the white light coming through the window and how it hits her face. Something about the bright fluorescent lights of the room— I feel like I am talking to an angel, and I confess to it, to her, "I... I think I believe in God."

Then she does something that changes my life. She smiles bigger than ever, gives me a look of complete acceptance, and then pats my head. My heart flutters, and for an instance, I feel like I have just died from happiness.

When they leave, pattering down the hallway, I sit down on my bed and write in my journal. In an instant, I am crying. My ears heat up, and my face flushes. My entire body feels warm, as if it is being wrapped in a blanket. In that instant, I feel all the good things in this world at once. They pour into my body like nectar, and at that point, I realize three things: that the depression is gone, that I need to write about this, and that I need to forgive my parents.

With the last five minutes I have left on my track phone I call my father and tell him that I love him and that I am sorry. He doesn't ask me any questions, and I tell him I have to go because my phone is about to die. When I hang up, my phone has exactly two minutes left.

After that, I take a long shower. It is the appropriate thing to do. When I climb into bed and curl up, my heart is still beating rapidly. I am not quite sure what just happened, but I know that it is good. I need to sleep now because when I wake up, I will be completely new.

I tell my nurse the next day that I want to write a book about my depression. However, I don't tell her anything about my sister being an angel—I don't want her to think I'm psychotic. Her eyes bulge and her voice oozes out with joy. "Oh my God, you need to go to the creative writing workshop we have today!" I tell her I will. After we talk, I retreat to my little cozy and work some more on the puzzle.

Soon the same nurse returns. The workshop is starting. "Um, I think want to work on this puzzle, instead," I respond.

"Oh?"

"Yeah, I just really like solving puzzles."

"Oh, well okay then," she says. Her eyes lose their shine and her lips turn into something between a smirk and a frown. "Have fun then!" Her footsteps fade down the hallway, and at last it is just me and pieces in quiet solitude.

Patients often stroll around the ward as a form of exercise. About twenty minutes later, Nick comes by and sits down beside me. As he approaches, I feel like an animal, watching another approach from a distance. I eye him up and down, watch his body movements and find no harm in him coming. "Are you purposefully not looking at the box?" he asks.

"What?" I glance at the floor and notice that the lid is turned over. "Oh, um, I guess I didn't think much about it."

After he leaves I make a conscious effort not to look at the solution. I like the suspense—it seems more realistic.

Tom wanders by soon afterwards. He offers to help with the puzzle some, jamming pieces together. We then start making animal noises and horrible melodies together. He doesn't contribute much, only managing to mush together pieces that don't belong to each other. I solve the rest of the puzzle and let him place the last piece. He is very proud of himself. Two days later, he is the first of us to get discharged.

They keep me for another week and a half. Part of it is because I'm having trouble deciding whether to return to school or head straight home. Another reason is because I have very good health insurance. On the last Monday, right before her flight, Chi Ti comes back to have a family meeting with my treatment team. I sit in the room and listen as they talk about my case. My sister says something which I can't forget, "I think that if My Ngoc goes back home, she could get a lot closer to her parents, which is something that I think could benefit her a lot."

The following morning, during the meeting with my team, I make my final announcement, "I think I want to..." I am about to tell them that I want to go back to school, but I pause. Chi Ti's words are repeating in my head. I think for a few seconds and continue, "I...I think it's time to do something different. What I was doing before wasn't working, and if I go back to school I will just fall back into the same pattern. I... I want to go home."

Dr. White-Bateman looks at me with a smile. Her eyes are bright, and she says, "I think you made the right decision."

I do very little the first month I am home. When I feel it was time, I emerge from the house and buy three puzzle sets of disparate difficulty. When it is late at night and I am too tired to write anymore, I go to my desk and sort out puzzle pieces until four in the morning. Some people prefer mornings. I prefer the late nights, when there is nothing, not even sunlight, to disrupt my thoughts.

A few months after I arrive home I receive my medical records in the mail. Towards the end of my report is a line that reads, "Several of the nurses had reported that My Ngoc sometimes has grandiose thoughts about her writing." I laugh out loud and file the paper away.

Now that I am back at school, I don't really have time to do puzzles. One night, however, I pass a girl in the dining hall working alone on a circular puzzle. She is gone by the time I come back, but I am delighted to see that the puzzle is still there. The circular borders are now pieced together.

Slowly, I put away my coat and sit in the chair, feeling like a traveler who has just arrived home from a long journey. My goal is to complete the entire puzzle. By midnight I have put together a third of it, but it is time for me to go. I have an anatomy quiz tomorrow, a bigger and far more complex puzzle to solve. Besides, the night guard would have sent me to bed by this time anyways if I were back in the hospital. So I leave, patting myself on the back for all those pieces I managed to put together.

Two days later, I see that someone else has solved the puzzle in the dining hall. I smile and wonder if the same girl put in the last piece. If it was her, I hope that she found whatever she was seeking and that when the final picture came together, it was beautiful.

CHAPTER 10

COUNTING CHANGE

The Looking and the Overlooked (2009)
Acrylic Newspaper, Chalk Pastel, Pennies, and Cloth on Wood
56 in x 36 in

"Công cha như núi Thái Sơn,
Nghĩa mẹ như nước trong nguồn chảy ra
Một lòng thờ mẹ kính cha,
Cho tròn chữ hiếu mới là đạo con.

A father's love like the tallest mountain
A mother's love like a river flowing from the deepest source
Always treasure mother and respect father
Obeying and understanding, a child's greatest fulfillment

    – Vietnamese Proverb

THERE ARE TWO TYPES of people in the world: those who pick up change and those who don't.

My father picks up every rusting coin he sees: the few dirty pennies under a cushion, the spare nickel in the left pocket of his work trousers. He brings them all home, and they go into the Tupperware container that he stores in the third right hand drawer next to his folded cotton underwear. When the Tupperware fills up, he pours the contents into the gallon-sized ice cream bucket. When the bucket fills, he counts his change.

Roughly one week after I return home from McLean, he comes into my room one night at around eleven, bringing the ice cream tub and the Tupperware, both overflowing with coins.

"Do you want to help me count these?"

It turns out that my mom has a stash of her own. Shortly after my dad drops off his coins, she beckons me into her closet and pulls out a plastic bag covered in dark rusty stains. "These too," she says.

I decide to count all the change that night, no matter how long it takes. Fortunately, my dad has some materials ready. A few years ago he had bought a coin sorter from Wal-Mart. He gives me this along with a pack of coin wrappers.

With mountains of change surrounding me on all sides, I take on my task, dropping my first few coins through the slot. The coins slide out slowly. The dimes sometimes fall into the wrong hole and land inside the penny stack. The pennies will go into the nickel slots, and I every minute or so I have to stop the machine and pull them out.

After a while, I do everything by hand, grabbing a handful of quarters and throwing them all into the slot. They come out, bit by bit, and stack up inside the paper rolls. By now I have fallen into a rhythm, placing about eleven quarters at a time into the slot, and rummaging around the pile of change for another handful while the machine sorts them.

I continue like this until midnight, and then half past midnight. The rolls of quarters pile up around me. Suddenly I hear a knock on the door. My dad comes in and asks me how I am doing. I show him the stacks. "I've gotten almost a hundred and fifty dollars!"

He kneels down beside me and inspects the coin machine. After a while, he looks up and says, "Whatever you can count is yours. This can be your Christmas gift."

"Really?"

He nods, smiling, and leaves soon after that.

I work for about another half hour until I hear footsteps thumping across the hardwood floors towards my bedroom. They stop short of the entrance and turn into series of furious knocks on the door. My mother. "Buoi!" she screams. "What the hell are you doing up this late? Do you want to harm your body? Do you want to get sick and go to the hospital again?"

She opens the door and comes in, hands on her hips, frowning down at me. All at once, I think of how insane I must look to her, how much she misunderstands my actions, and how impossible it will be to explain why I have to count this change tonight.

"Mom, please let me count this change!" I scream. "I'm not hurting anyone."

"You are so stupid! Did you even hear what I said? Do this tomorrow morning. Do you know what time it is?"

"Why can't you just leave me alone?"

It is pointless. She knows she is right, and I know I am being wronged. I don't want to give up my stance, so I scream and shout and argue until she throws up her hands and leaves. "You never listen to me anymore. I'm such a horrible mother. I can't teach my kids anything. *Ayaah!*" Another sigh, followed by the slam of the door, and then a stinging silence.

When I am sure she has retreated back to her bedroom, I turn the machine back on and let its electric hum fill up the silence. The sounds feel forced and awkward. It *is* late, I admit, but not any later than I would be staying up if I were in college.

Not to my surprise, she comes back an hour later when it is nearing two in the morning. This time, her voice is less willing to cooperate. She yells at me with a hoarse and low grumble, a mix between a whisper and a scream. I am scared inside, but I will not give up—I am doing more than just counting change.

After this I know that she is gone for good. I am grateful for the peace, though I am beaten on the inside. Again, the machine starts, but I quickly turn it off because the noise is giving me a headache. I continue with the quarters, though this time, I just stack them in my hands and place them into the slots.

By two thirty in the morning I have fallen into a sort of meditation, picking up the quarters, dropping them in. The cool touch of metal and the sounds of coins hitting each other turn to memories inside my head.

Years ago, when she was still in high school, Chi Ti loved to collect quarters. She kept any quarters that had the background of a different state other than Georgia. The government only released a few new states every year, however, so we waited in anticipation for the sudden appearance of any new coins whenever my sister dumped out the next batch of change from her piggy bank.

Several days before her seventeenth birthday, I went to Wal-Mart and purchased a map of the America using the money I saved up from my allowance. Each state had a hole the size of a quarter. It would be the perfect gift.

That night, Chi Ti and I sat on her bed inserting a quarter in each hole. Sometimes she let me place them in, but most of the time she did the work because she knew how to align the quarters perfectly. We went through all the quarters and saw that half of the country was still missing coins.

After that, every few months we would find a couple of new quarters to place on the map. The Eastern states got filled first; Rhode Island was the last of them. After that came the Midwest, then further out to California, New Mexico, and at last, Alaska and Hawaii.

Then everything stopped. The map filled up, Chi Ti went off to college and I had my first boyfriend. My sister had begun to keep her own secrets long before I learned to withhold my world from her. All I knew was that the sister whose face glowed with excitement with every new quarter was gone. In her place was a stone-faced woman who knew no surprises and carried only a harsh mouth and criticizing eyes.

The last memories I had with her were not pleasant ones.

When she came to visit me in the hospital we sat face to face in the cafeteria; she eyed me with suspicion and said, almost accusingly, with her hands folded together on the table, "Do you have, like, a brain disorder or something?"

Later on she offered her advice multiple times on the phone: "Do you know how completely selfish you are to even think of suicide? Why do you think you need to go back home? You're just being lazy, aren't you? You know what you are? You are weak. You see your friends—they don't have to go to the hospital. They're doing fine, so why can't you?"

During conversations like those I tried to stay on the phone as long as I could to explain myself: "Ti, I'm not going back home because I'm lazy. It's almost the end of the semester, and if I go back I'll be so behind, and everyone's going to be super stressed and I'll be all alone again." I plead to her. "And there are so many kids at school who need help too, they just don't talk about it."

"I don't care. I think all those kids who are depressed are just spoiled. Mom and dad aren't paying twenty grand a semester for you to just take it easy and do whatever you want. You need to harden up and get your act together."

"Ti, they're not paying that much, just half of that."

"Don't you try to be smart with me Buoi. We're not paying for you to go to school to get all educated just so you get talk back to us. It seems to me that you just aren't strong enough to handle Harvard. If you take this year off, come back, and *still* can't deal with it, then I think you should just transfer to college back home. I know you're not liking what I'm saying, but I still think you should have listened to me and gone to UNC instead."

After this I just hung up and burst into tears.

I shake the image from my head. Some memories are best left alone.

By now all the quarters have been sorted into the paper containers. I turn to the dimes, and then to the nickels, and at last the pennies. When it turns four in the morning I have to stop, but in the morning I resume with the same intensity as last night, working from the moment I open my eyes until the early afternoon, when, at last, all of the change, save for a few pennies which cannot fit, have been sorted and counted.

The rolls take up the entirety of a large shoebox that weighs almost forty pounds. The teller at the bank takes the box behind the counter and says, "Lord, did you count all these by yourself? I'd be bored to death if I had to do this. It's something I'd do in front of the TV, you know."

I tell her that I in fact did count all the change by myself. "I find it rather meditative."

The total comes to four hundred eighty four dollars and fifty cents. The banker throws away the shoebox for me and hands me a deposit slip. With the weight of all that change off my shoulders, I leave the bank and head home, feeling considerably lighter and richer than I was before.

CHAPTER 11

THE DROP

"Love her as in childhood
Through feeble, old and grey.
For you'll never miss a mother's love
Till she's buried beneath the clay."

– Frank McCourt, *Angela's Ashes*

A sweet old lady, smiling and dressed in pastel floral patterns, sits smiling at me from her chair. I fumble around, gathering the necessary tools for my first real operation. This is all part of my new part time job as a research assistant in a geriatric clinic. So far I've learned that I enjoy spending time with old people.

After two months at home, I was ready to interact with the outside world again. It was time to be an adult and hold responsibilities to society. To prove myself ready to return to Harvard, I would have to maintain a full-time schedule for at least six months, gather letters of recommendation from my bosses and then write a statement of reflection. All students on medical leave have to do this. I chose to work in a clinical setting because, after everything that happened, I wanted to become a psychiatrist, and this was the first step of a long journey.

I started out dealing with just paperwork, but when my boss saw that I was capable of doing more than filing patient charts, she let me run the visits.

This lady is a part of our study on atrial fibrillation. During the sessions we are required to measure the thickness of their blood by giving an INR, short for international normalized ratio blood test. I am almost done prepping for my first one.

I slowly put on my gloves and sit down on the stool in front of the lady. Everything happens very quickly. I sanitize her hands, take out the gauze and a Band-Aid in preparation, remove the stinger from its packet, and before I can think I have already punctured a hole in her—blood, the sweet red nectar is pouring from her finger.

I have watched blood flow from my body countless times. I am consistently taken back by its color, its silent movement across my skin, its slight saltiness against my tongue. Most of the time, I am not expecting it or the events causing it, unless if I need to have it drawn. But even then, my own blood is quarantined inside tubes and I am not called to interact with it.

That situation did come, when I had purposefully take blood from my own body.

In the beginning of my sophomore year in college, the same year I had my breakdown, I took a basic science in which we studied the nature of certain molecules essential to life. Often, we researched the diseases associated with the molecules, so when we reached insulin, we turned our heads to diabetes.

In a class lab, we had to measure our blood-sugar levels before and after eating a glucose tablet. To do this we would have to prick our fingers with a tiny needle, wait for the blood to come out and then insert that droplet onto the test strip of a machine for measurement. It was quite simple, really, but the instructions did prepare me for the emotional experience.

There were only a few pricking machines, so we had to share. I sat at my desk and watched ten other students play with their blood. The class, which generally stayed apathetically silent, was erupting into giggles and shouts of delight. I watched a tall lean boy next to me grin and stare cross-eyed at his finger as the blood came out. Another girl in the back yelled to the class that she had a lot of blood in her finger. I secretly prayed that I would get a lot of blood too. What if it didn't come out? What if there wasn't enough blood?

The machine finally came to me. With the needle poised and ready to shoot, I counted to three and then pressed down hard on the release button. Before I could make sense of the pain it was gone. I looked down, and to my delight, a small drop had already formed form at the side of my finger. It swelled to twice its size and turned slightly darker in hue. I let it drip onto the testing strip of the machine and, once it was done reading, handed it to my friend.

Barely anything came out from his fingers. I watched him scrape the side of his finger against the plastic strip in order to get any few drops in, but it was not enough, and the machine showed a failed reading. He tried again, pricking himself from a different finger, but only a tiny drop went out. The machine revealed the same result: FAIL.

I stared more than I should have — I felt sorry for him. And yet, it wasn't because he couldn't draw blood, but because it seemed as though his body did not hold any blood, as if it had failed to keep itself running.

In the meantime, a giant drop of blood had already swelled on my skin and was threatening to trickle down my finger. It wouldn't stop coming out, and I continually wiped the drops away only to find them quickly replaced by another.

I was amazed at how much blood I had. More so, I was surprised at the vividness of its color. Seeing so much of my own blood, I felt pride.

The same feeling overwhelms me when I see this woman's blood gush up from the puncture in her finger, forming a perfect round droplet. As I milk her finger for more blood, collecting it into the cup as I went, it spreads to different parts of her finger, collecting in the small rivets of her skin. Wherever it goes it leaves behind the same familiar crimson stain. I no longer feel like I am dealing with a foreign object. Her skin is now my skin, her blood my blood.

Once I have filled the cup with enough blood, I insert it into the cuvette, which drains the blood and simmers it. I watch the blood boil.

I think her blood looks normal, but when the test results come back, we see that her INR has climbed up to almost five since the last session. The normal range is two to three. I don't know what that means—her blood could have either been too thick or too thin. If it is too thin, her blood might run like liquid through her body and seeping out in every little hole—through her eyes, her ears, her pores. If it is too thick, it can clot and stick to the vessels. Perhaps her high body temperature will heat up the blood, just like the machine did to the sample, and simmer it softly, just until it is cooked and dark brown like the coagulated pork blood sold in Vietnamese grocery stores. No matter the case, I feel like a tidal wave had just hit me. I cannot believe that I have touched someone so close to death.

Human skin is not very thick—just two to three millimeters wide, and yet it manages to hide the color of our bodies. If we peel off our skins and throw them in a corner, all that remains will be piles of meat and bone complete with a set of eyeballs and spilling organs. And surrounding that is blood, expanses of blood in all directions, for each human body contains up to five quarts of blood, enough to cover and stain the hardwood floor of any kitchen.

Blood itself holds within it the history of an entire life, and as long as we live, it flows through our bodies carrying evidence of our past, making us bleed and clot and cry until one day that history suddenly dissipates, and blood withers away with the life that it once carried.

Whenever one of our patients has a bleed event or is hospitalized for any reason, we receive pages and pages of lab results measuring almost every imaginable chemical in their blood. I have to enter each value into the computer: the time and date the blood was collected, the chemical being measured, and its normal range. It takes hours and hours to enter hundreds of lab values.

We receive an emergency case one morning. I pull out the patient's file in preparation for my data entry. This is my first time looking closely at any medical terms. Some words I understand right away, such as uric acid, glucose and sodium. Other words I come to understand in time, like *RBC* for red blood cells, *WBC* for white blood cells and *hgb* for hemoglobin. Still there are words that I have never seen before and still can't comprehend, and in these cases I can only tell if they are out of range. It turns out that almost all of his values are abnormal.

The dates for these lab results run from December 28 to January 6. The levels are mostly normal in December, but come January 2, almost half of his *Lymph%*'s and *MCV*'s and *MPV*'s are slightly abnormal, and then by January 6 his glucose levels have jumped to five times the normal amount.

But I am finally done, and I think no more about it. I simply assume that everyone is a bit off in some way or another.

Later on, as I hand the paperwork back to my boss, I mention how a lot of his labs are completely out of range. She pauses for a second and then explains that this patient has been in the hospital for quite some time for a serious bleeding event. She has been quietly watching him die.

I realize that I have just succeeded in documenting the slow death of a man by watching his blood become berserk on paper. Like how the lights on a switchboard slowly go out one by one in a crashing plane, increasing in speed until all of a sudden the lights go out all at once, I am watching the switches go out for every vital fluid in this man's body. One by one, the chemicals slip out of range until the day all of his blood is out of control. Then that last light will turn black, and he will have hit the end.

I sit in front of the computer with no more blood to enter. A few days after, we receive a safety notification letter from the International Review Board, saying that the cause of concern was, in cold, bold letters, DEATH. I punch holes in that document and file it away in the binder used specifically for study correspondence, and then put that stark white paper away until it is time to move onto the next life

CHAPTER 12

THE SUNFLOWER

James (2011)
Chalk Pastel on Paper
18 in x 24 in

"If you have lost your smile and yet are still capable of seeing that a dandelion is keeping it for you, the situation is not too bad. You still have enough mindfulness to see that the smile is there."

—Thich Nhat Hanh, *Peace is Every Step*

"The wound is the place where the Light enters you."

– Rumi

MY THERAPIST STARES AT ME through her thick-rimmed glasses. Looking meditative and concerned, she says, softly, "Sometimes you can be too hard on yourself My Ngoc. This is not easy, and you've made so much progress in such little time."

Progress. What a strange word. What can it possibly mean? Lately, I've been able to sleep without having night terrors in which I am being eaten alive, possessed by demons or killing my own family. I am not crying myself to sleep every night. I can also "handle the stresses of daily life" and "engage in healthy social interactions" without having sudden urges to cry or ram my head against the wall. Most importantly, the thoughts of death have more or less gone away. Whereas before I walked around campus with an eternal spell of death on my forehead, thinking of jumping whenever I was up high or getting myself into near-death situations whenever I rode my bike, I can go for weeks now without the thought of killing myself.

I have made progress in that I am not who I was back in November, when I was first diagnosed with Major Depressive Disorder. I left Harvard with the mission of starting a new life, and for the past few months dedicated all my energy to this healing process. I am still on antidepressants, still going through therapy. Instead of a suicide plan, I have a plan of treatment, and that plan is both progress and the path to progress.

The first few months were good. I thought that if I fought depression with all my might and focused all of my energy to healing, that all these problems would be cleared right away. Optimism and impatience drove me forward, but now I feel myself sinking again.

My work at the clinic no longer feels inspiring. The repetition of work drags me down. The reality of life after college seems so decrepit and monotonous, and I am lonelier than ever, more separated than my friends who are in college. While the care and attention of my parents used to touch me, their remaining concern only fills me with the conviction that there is indeed something still horribly wrong with me, something that will never go away.

"I'm tired of all this," I say. "Ever since my breakdown, everything has been about this goddamn depression and getting better and re-accessing my entire life and trying to explain everything to everyone. I want to just get away from it all and go to a country where no one knows me, like I did last summer, but I know I can't… because that would just be running away from my problems, so now I'm stuck here. I'm trying my best, but… but I'm just so, so *tired* of it all."

"Maybe you can try doing something completely unrelated, like taking a flower arranging course. You know, and get your mind off of things for a while."

She has a point.

The moment I come home I grab my computer and look up classes that I can take. There are no flower arranging courses, but I find a list of evening courses and art seminars in Atlanta. I give up on this when I see how much each class costs. I will have to pay hundreds of dollars to learn something that I can easily teach myself at home. Also, I know that none of the courses will compare to the rigor of the classes I took at Harvard. So that's the end of that.

Exasperated, I sit back and wonder what I can possibly do. My mind is about to spiral downwards when I remember the lima beans.

Earlier in the year, after church, Chi Nhung asked me to get some seeds.

"We need some seeds, Buoi!" she said. "You know, really big seeds that you can see from far away. You know, they're like, really big? Do you know what I'm talking about?"

"Uh, you mean lima beans?" I said.

"I don't know. I just need really, really big seeds."

"I think they're lima beans."

"Are you sure?"

"No."

"Buoi, you need to be sure. This is for *church*!" She looked at me desperately.

"Yeah, I'm pretty sure." I said. It had been ages since I had ever touched a lima bean. The last time I dealt with them was when I accidentally broke the stem of Chi Ti's plant that she was growing for the science fair. After four weeks, it had grown into a thick green stub with no leaves, like a diseased finger poking out of the ground. I tripped over the pot one day and sent the thing to its doom. After a thorough preaching from my sister, I never touched lima beans again.

Chi Nhung stared at me with her eyebrows furrowed together for a while. "Okay then. Why don't you get the beans? I don't know how to get them. What are they called again?"

"Lima beans."

"Ah... Okay, get the lima beans and bring them to church next week so I can make the videos of the kids pretending to plant the seeds and pray for them. After that, do you think you can grow them in time? You're really good with plants!"

"Yeah, I'll plant them."

"Great!" she said, and then looked at me again, "Are you sure they're called lima beans?"

"Yeah," I said, a bit unsure, "I'm sure."

After rehearsal, I went home and began my project. I took out a small plastic bag, placed a wet towel in it, and then, one by one, placed the seeds on the inside. I had done this before in the tenth grade when I grew a bunch of lettuce seeds for the science fair. I put the seeds on the table, where they could soak up the light from the big window.

The next morning, at work, I told Lisa, an older coworker, about my lima beans. "I'm growing some lima beans," I said. "They're for church." I was waiting for her to tell her how great it was to grow lima beans.

She was wearing some dark blue scrubs and had a pin over her left breast with the words "I ♥ CHURCH." We were eating chicken wraps. "That's so great," she said.

"Yeah, I know right," I said. "I hope they grow."

They didn't grow. Almost a week went by, and none of the seeds had even germinated. I even prayed for the seeds, but that didn't make them grow any faster. When the day of the performance came and the pots were still bare and black, my sister and I just stuck celery sticks in each pot.

We handed out the pots to all the kids who would be performing, and they asked me if these plants were for them. I knew that the plants would die under their care, but I couldn't bear taking prized possessions from children, so I let them keep the pots.

When my sister handed me a bag full of the same pots I had given away earlier, I was quite surprised. I didn't ask how or why she had gotten the plants, but I didn't care. I was glad to have them back.

A few nights later, I removed the seeds from the soil, curious to see if they had germinated. I plucked one seed from its base and was amazed to see that it had grown an inch-long root! I quickly checked all the other pots and squealed out loud when I saw that ten of them had grown long, thick roots. I got really excited and then forgot about it all.

With these memories fresh in my head, I think—if ten lima beans are enough to stimulate me, then I can have a whole orgasm of pleasure from growing an entire garden. They must still be there.

I go downstairs and check on the lima beans. They had grown stems and leaves!

I drive straight to Wal-Mart and pick out all the things that I want to grow: watermelon, cantaloupe, cilantro, broccoli, okra, and sunflowers.

All the seeds go into plastic bags later that evening. I clear the whole kitchen counter and make a place for my plants. This is going to be their home. I could have just put them in the soil and waited a week for them to emerge, but I can't do that. I want to be there for them right from the beginning, before they even knew what the world is, and watch them every step of the way.

And then I think—I'll keep a log of all of this like I did five years ago for the science fair! I'll keep track of every single detail and document every change in plans. I'll even initial and date besides every correction that I make, just like how I have to with my job!

I find an old composition notebook and write in big bold letters, "PROJECT GARDEN" on the front. I then set out to work, sketching out the shape and physical description of each seed, noting its quality and jotting down the plant's growth period and ideal temperature range. On the surface of each bag I count exactly how many seeds will be germinating for each type of plant as well as all my plans on when to transfer them to a geoponic system. I know that this is just bullshit science, but I don't care—I'm too happy.

When I wake up, and before I leave for work, check the bags to see if any new growth has occurred. For two days, nothing happens. The seeds have only gotten squishier. Some of the darker ones, like watermelon, have stained the paper towel with a disturbing brown color.

But then, on the third day, I see a change in the broccoli. Something white is protruding from the outer covering. It takes me five whole seconds to recognize that it is actually a root. I had my skepticisms before, because I had no idea how such any plant could fit inside such a small seed, but now it is happening before my eyes.

"Look mom! I used to be this size!" I say as I show my mom the seeds. "And look—I turned out to be so much smarter than the broccoli!"

The days go by. I make sure to water the plants every night. My hopes grow along with them, and I become more and more hopeful about my situation in general until one day, it hits me again. One night in late February, I lose control of my emotions and made another death wish. The next day, I can't do anything. When I finally wake up, it is drizzling outside, the whole day has almost gone by, and I have to miss work. I go downstairs to check on my plants but can only notice how small and pathetic they look, just like me.

My mom sees my sadness and walks up beside me. "When I was little, I had a gift, like you do, with words," she says. "There is this one poem that I still remember." She tells the story of a sad little boy and a bean plant. The boy walks into a garden and sees the little bean plants growing. They are extremely frail, but he notices how determined they are to live, and how they grow only towards the sun. He sees all this, and he no longer feels sad.

A strange love comes upon me. I can't waste time while the lives I created need protection and nourishment. I thank my mom for the story, put away my sadness and set out to prepare my garden.

It takes hours of hoeing and digging in the rain, but I don't stop. I loosen up the soil, mix it and arrange it in rows, ready-made homes for all my little babies. I set my plants free. I know it's going to be great. I envision a luscious garden frothing with leaves and flowers and fruit.

Two weeks later, they all die.

Several days of intense rain and a sudden cold spell prove more than enough to wipe out all the little lives. I step outside to find out that a giant massacre has silently taken place overnight. I check all the places where all my little children had been, and all I see is dried plant carcasses. The cracked, barren soil mocks me, and I laugh—I have to or otherwise I'd cry. Perhaps it was a bit silly of me to think that I would actually have a thriving garden in the middle of February. After all, grandiose thoughts are a sign of bipolar disorder.

But there is one plant that survived—a tiny little sunflower.

Of all the plants, I expected this one to die first, as it was broken at the stem when I put it in the ground. Having noticed this, I supported it with extra soil on all sides. This very soil had kept the plant incubated and aligned throughout the changes in weather.

I decide that this as a miracle plant and set my heart out to keep it alive for as long as I could. After all, we are kindred spirits. We both have been through hard times, and we have both recovered from our situation with a lot of help from loved ones. And since we both are going to be rooted in Georgia, we might as well take care of each other and grow stronger together, growing only towards the light.

CHAPTER 13

THE WALK

Field of Yellow Flowers (2012)
Acrylic on Canvas
24 in x 18 in

"Perhaps we should never procure a new suit, however ragged or dirty the old, until we have so conducted, so enterprised or sailed in some way, that we feel like new men in the old, and that to retain it would be like keeping new wine in old bottles."

— Henry David Thoreau, *Walden*

I WALK IN SILENCE next to my sister. After sharing dinner together at a local café, where the cook put too much salt in my noodles, we thought it would be a good idea to walk off our meal on the famous suspension bridge in Charleston. Ever since she got her new job as a hospital management engineer, I've driven down this bridge many times coming up to visit her. This is the first time that I get a chance to traverse it by foot. It's a new experience for both of us as well as a way to get her mind out of misery, which is really the entire reason why I am up in Charleston in the first place.

A month before I was scheduled to return to Harvard, Chi Ti gave me a call right after midnight. We had not talked in weeks. From the way she said "hello" I immediately knew something was terribly wrong. When I heard her voice over the phone, the resentment washed away, leaving only room for concern in my heart. She had just broken up with her boyfriend, and she was at an emergency low. The next day I quit my internship at the International Rescue Committee, where I had been driving recent refugees to their doctors' appointments, to go up to Charleston and take care of her.

During the first two days, my sister lay debilitated on her couch. I spoon-fed her ramen noodles and sang her to sleep. Gradually I shifted my focus on the more complicated process of healing the mind. So far I've redesigned her apartment, hung up paintings, threw away unwanted memories, and reorganized her closets. When that project was done I took her to a comedy club, cooked elaborate meals, played badminton with her, and helped her pick out a new bike.

I have to keep reminding myself that healing takes time. It takes at least two months to feel better after a breakup, I tell her, and it has only been three weeks since she broke up with her boyfriend.

I think of all the things I can say to make her feel better, but we've already talked about the same things several times during this walk. "I fucked up so bad," she says. "I can't believe I was such a monster," she adds. "I don't see a future."

The conversation is also turning out less successful than I anticipated. On top of that, every step brings on a pain that shoots up from the bottom of my feet, and after several hundred lacerations on the heel, this walk has become less enjoyable. I guess if it hurts, it has to hurt.

In the car, I take off my sandals and inspect the soles. After so much wear, the soles have thinned out and compressed down to the frame inside. The metal grid, clearly shown by now, had been biting into my flesh with every step.

"You should probably throw those shoes away. They're hurting you, for Christ's sake," says my sister. She has a point.

When we arrive home I proceed to throw them all away. First to go is the pair of black flats. I bought them during the fall of my freshman year from the Urban Outfitters in Harvard Square. White strings hang out from every seam, covering up the intricate lace designs that had once been so elegant. I close my eyes and gave them one last "thank you" before I let them clunk to the bottom of the trashcan. They had looked so good with my white cotton dress.

Next to go is the pair of Nike tennis shoes. They had accompanied me when I went to my first gym in college. After that first year was over, they traveled with me across South America and up the peaks of Machu Picchu. The original light grey fabric had turned a permanent brown after walking through so much mud and dirt. I had scrubbed them many times, but the history of their journeys refused to be washed away.

I give my last thank you to this pair as well before dropping them in the bin.

I pick up the pair of gray sandals and prepare to part with them. I wonder if I will ever be able to find another pair like these. They have a simple design—a single strap that wraps around the ankle for support and two additional straps that run along the top of the foot. In the middle stands a single large rose made of twisted leather. The tips of the petals have zippers on them, which makes the shoe look elegant, modern, and edgy.

My heart breaks a bit as I let them go, but I tell myself that it is necessary to say goodbye. As painful as this breakup is, it is not my first. These shoes are actually a replacement for an earlier pair of golden shoes, so I am used to the process of moving on.

However, I have never before been in a circumstance when all of my most favorite shoes are suddenly thrown away. A void has appeared where the shoes once were—a place in my heart that held so many memories—I enter a sort of crisis.

No more time can be wasted. I can only go around wearing my sister's old flip-flops for so long. The next day my sister picks me up after work and takes me to get some new shoes.

We go through several shopping centers before we find a promising store. I walk up and down the aisles for half an hour, picking up one shoe, finding another. I try on black pairs, white pairs, and grey pairs. Some of them feature neon shoelaces, others aerodynamic soles. In my mind, however, I can only reminisce of the simplicity of the old design—soft gray shades with a single pink swish, complete with a thin, white underlining. Everything else is too complicated and overdone.

During my search I come across my old shoe. A wave of nostalgia overcomes me, and I am tempted to buy it again. But I tell myself that I need to move on from the past, that it is possible to find a better pair.

After spending an hour in the store, my mind becomes overloaded. In my indecision I have to perform the inevitable shopping algorithm that weighs all the possible designs and combinations that will give me the most happiness out of a shoe. This equation becomes necessary in circumstances when my heart has not found its chosen item, and my brain has to do all the work.

Just as we are about to leave, I see a pair on display near the bottom of the shelf that had previously gone unnoticed. A pause, an inhale, and I step over and try them on. So far, nothing about the shoe repulses me. It is a medium shade of gray in color. They have the pink swish on the exterior sides and a smaller, silver logo on the inside. Instead of white bottoms, which my previous pair had, these shoes sport pink soles. But there is something else—these shoes have a small shear section of cloth, which reveals a zigzag of pink leather. This final touch makes the shoes look not only elegant, but also sexy. I know I don't need to do any more calculations then. I have found my pair.

Next on the list is to replace my flats. I know what I really want is a casual pair of closed toed shoes, so I consider getting a pair of loafers. We make a stop at TJ Maxx, and it takes less than three minutes for me to find them. I walk through the automatic doors, head straight for the shoe section and enter the aisle for women's size seven. I give the shelves a cursory run over, my eyes skipping over any pair of sandals, high heels, pumps, flip flops that I saw. With this filter in my eyes, the pair of light tan

Michael Khorr's shoes shines through among the masses. They are the last surviving species of their kind in the entire section. It is almost too easy to be true.

By then, it is roughly 8:45 PM, and store will be closing in fifteen minutes. Seeing that we still have a bit of time left, my sister suggests we go to next door to Marshall's for one last investigation. After all, I still need to replace the pair of sandals.

I doubt I can possibly be any happier after finding two perfect shoes in a row, but I decide to follow my lucky streak.

We enter yet another pair of automatic doors, and, again, I head straight towards the shoe section in the back. I browse aisle by aisle, my heart beating loudly inside my ear. I see a pair or two that look promising, but none of them speak to me. So I continue stalking. When I turn a third corner, I see in a distance, towards the end of the racks, a glimmer of gold. My heart stops as I come closer and closer. Can this be it?

On display is a set of golden sandals. They have shiny metal straps. One goes behind the heel and another wraps around the top of the foot. In the center are three metal stars, joined together by metal clasps. It reminds me of Russian gypsies and princesses and mermaids. But there is more. They also have blue stones between each flower and at the center of each flower.

I adjust the straps around my feet, letting them snap into place. The metal flowers slide across my skin and rest, cool and glimmering on my feet. At that moment I know exactly how Cinderella felt as her feet nested into her glass slippers—a sense of wonder and completion. I scream to my sister, "Oh my God, I've come full circle!"

That night, I sit on the carpet and display all my new shoes in front of me. They make a varied and unique team, like a multicultural group of superheroes. My sister also gives me two pairs of her high heels: a pair of fur lined ankle boots and a pair of skin-colored heels with elaborate straps wrapping the foot. I can wear these whenever I need some sass, be it hot or cold weather. Whenever I want to look scholarly and classic, I can wear my boat shoes. Whenever I need go to fast, I have my tennis shoes to help me on my missions. Whenever it is warm and sunny, I can whip out my golden shoes and walk, like a shining queen.

"Let me take a picture of you and your shoes!" says my sister. She helps me arrange them and then snaps some photos. "Wait, put the boots closer to you!"

Her voice is so sweet and kind. This is who she really is, a kind and beautiful woman who had become calloused by hurt. This recent pain had broken down all her walls and shattered her to the deepest chamber of her heart. At first she lay fragile and helpless, debilitated at the realization of what she had done and who she had been, but in breaking down she was able to star over anew. Sometimes you have to destroy everything to build something better. Now that we both know what it feels like to be frail and healing, we are finding some common ground with each other again, and it feels good.

It's been five years since I've felt this close to my sister. The shoes that I threw away were all the shoes I had walked in during the times of separation between us. After several years, they have led me here to her little apartment in Charleston, where we sit at her small round dining table and whisper over mugs of green tea in the mornings and sit in silence by the lake at night. I can only imagine where I'll be and who I'll be with when these new shoes have done their work.

CHAPTER 14

WHAT KIND OF HEART

Black Cloth (2012)
Charcoal on Newsprint
20 in x 18 in

"He had the strangest feeling that there was someone standing right behind the veil on the other side of the archway. Gripping his wand very tightly, he edged around the dais, but there was nobody there; all that could be seen was the other side of the tattered black veil."

— JK Rowling, *Harry Potter and the Prisoner of Azkaban*

"In the depth of winter I finally learned that there was in me an invincible summer."

— Albert Camus

ON COLD, SNOWY DAYS, I like to lie in my bed, wrapped up in my blankets as if in a womb, and stare at the lights suspended above me. It is my first semester back at school, and I have made it past November. Outside the snow blankets the houses in a white carpet, and I am inside feeling safe and warm. My bed is a home for me, a most special place to return to, so I have turned it into a nest. Christmas lights hang above my bed on top of the canopy made from an old bed sheet. At night, when only the Christmas lights are turned on, the ceiling above resembles a constellation in the night sky.

There is a string of lights that does not make it above the canopy. It ascends from the socket and up the wall, towards the ceiling before it disappears behind the sheets. From far away these lights resemble dozens of fireflies, frozen in motion.

Now, I lie in bed with my glasses off. I purposefully take away my vision when I do not want to focus on anything in particular. I like to know that I can choose when I want to participate in the world. My gaze shifts to the string of lights—they have lost their pointed shape and become floating orbs with bright cores and faded halos at the edges.

My body feels like it is floating on the sheets, and my eyes see but do not stare at anything in particular. I start to lose my sense of time when the lights suddenly start pulsing.

The halos expand and shrink repeatedly. Each time the white core grows in intensity and causes the sphere to increase to about twice its size. Soon afterwards, it shrinks temporarily, and then bursts out again in fits, first after a short pause, and then a longer pause. A thought comes to my mind—can it be that the lights are pulsating at the same rhythm as my heart? Could it be that with each pump, the extra blood flow to my eyes makes the cells more receptive to light?

I press my hand above my heart and listen, watching the lights as I feel for my pulse. It is indeed true! I stay like this for a few more minutes, wide-eyed, mesmerized.

I know a few things about the human heart, probably more than most people do, from my current course in human anatomy. In class I have gotten to place my thumb through the vena cava of a calf's fresh and bleeding heart and run a scalpel through the cat's left ventricle. Even more so, I know the science behind the mechanics of the human heart, which had before only existed as a barely audible thump. I am astonished to know that my heart has changed over the years—from the moment I was born.

This is what I have learned: that babies don't have working lungs—they cannot breathe. The lungs sag within the chest of the baby as limp sacs, only getting enough oxygen to maintain basic metabolic processes. Inside the womb, the only oxygen that the baby gets comes directly from the mother's blood. The heart does not, cannot pump blood to the lungs, because the pressure within the lungs is too great.

To make up for this, the heart has developed holes that allow the blood to bypass the lungs. The first one, called the *foramen ovule*, lies between the two atria so that blood, upon entering the heart, can skip its normal route—from the right atrium to the right ventricle, into the left ventricle, through the lungs, and back into the left atrium—and head directly to the left atrium. The other hole is the *ductus arteriosis*, which connects the pulmonary artery with the aorta. Any blood that does not flow through the foramen ovale gets shunted here directly to the aorta, where it can circulate throughout the body.

At birth, everything changes.

The moment a baby comes into the world, its lungs inflate, blowing up like airbags in a car crash. Air rushes down the trachea, branching into the bronchioles, down the hundreds of bronchiole, and into the millions of tiny alveolar sacs. The body senses that the lungs are now working, and it changes the heart to accommodate this new system. A flap immediately closes down on the foramen ovule, sealing the hole permanently. The ductus arteriosis fades away on its own, hardening into a ligament. By the end of the second day, it is completely gone. The baby cries when this happens, but it never stops breathing. Miraculously, it learns to live, and the lungs stay inflated.

My body did all of this without even giving me notice.

After a few minutes, I throw myself under the covers, separating myself from this spectacular. I think of the blood gushing into my eyeballs, washing over each and every cell behind my retina. This is a breakthrough, I say to myself. I need to confirm that this phenomenon is true, so I crawl out of the covers again and continue staring at the lights. After a few seconds, my eyes manage to unfocused their gaze, and the little balls move again: the same pattern, ceaselessly dancing along to a heart that never fails.

That same class has taught me that a single heart will beat the exact same number of times in a life regardless of the host's size or shape: The tree shrew's heart beats roughly three-hundred-sixty times every minute for two and a half years; the elephant's heart twenty times per minute for fifty-seven; and the dog's heart eighty times a minute for twelve years. Each heart beats roughly five hundred million times in a given lifetime. Why? Because all hearts are made of the same stuff.

Human hearts beat for longer thanks to technology and medicine. Ours beats an average of sixty-five times every minute for minute for seventy-five years, totaling in about 2,500 million beats in a lifetime. Yet, this life is only prolonged, not guaranteed, and we die once our bodies are used up. Even the most noble-hearted pass away.

Another thought comes into my mind, and this time, it is not of hearts or science, but of Lhasa, a singer. I discovered her voice a year ago and was heart broken to find that she had already passed away. Just a few weeks ago I watched a video of her performing live.

The images replay themselves now in my head:

"And here is a singer who was born to a Mexican father and an American mother." The announcer prepares his audience, "and who will run off to perform in a circus every now and then. Everyone, meet Lhasa."

It is hard, if not impossible to put Lhasa under one label. She spent her childhood traveling back and forth the Mexican-American border on a converted school bus. Her parents, hippies at the time, did not name her until she was five months old, when her mother encountered the word Lhasa while reading a book on Tibet and thought it was the most beautiful name imaginable.

The lady comes onto the stage, and she speaks, "My father is a great storyteller. But he doesn't tell stories which he simply hears—he tells stories that he's thought of over many years." There is something immediately spectacular about her voice.

Some people believe that the voice comes directly from the soul. If this were true, Lhasa's soul would have come from some place very deep.

"When we're conceived," she goes on, "we appear in our mother's womb, more like a tiny infinite and tiny little light that just appears in the middle of this dark space that feels like an infinite night." She speaks slowly and deliberately, cherishing each word, which passes through her mouth. Her words rhyme, but she is not aware of it. "But slowly we're growing, and as we grow, little by little, we begin to feel sensations. And we begin to patch the walls of this place what we found ourselves in, and slowly we begin to hear sounds and feel socks and vibrations of things that come outside of our mother, who is moving and walking and running."

"And we can slowly hear that voice. And we keep on growing and growing and growing. And finally, the place that we are in, which was infinitely big, becomes smaller, and we have to be born. My father remembers the moment of his birth. The moment of birth is so violent and chaotic that all of us at that moment think 'I'm dying.' That this is the end of my life."

"And then, what a big surprise," says Lhasa.

"And we come out, and it's just beginning. And in the beginning we are very small, and the world looks infinitely bid, and we slowly learn to use our senses. We learn how to touch the contours of our new home. And how to use our senses. We learn how to use our eyes and ears and touch, but sometimes mixed in with everything, sometimes we hear sounds and feel shocks that come from somewhere outside of this life. And that other outside is just on the other side of a thin wall that is also transparent. And sounds can cross through, all through our lives. We hear things that are just like a memory, a reminder of something. And then, finally, this body becomes very uncomfortable too, and we have to die."

"And then we think to ourselves again—this is it. This is the end of me. But my father says it's just the moment when we go through the very thin transparent wall. Something we've done before. And we go on with something else. He also says that in the same way in which when are in our mother's womb, we are developing organs that we have no use for an they feel kind of awkward to us. We don't really know what to do with them, but they are there for later.

"So I, I'm going to sing you a song, which is how I imagined it would be later. It's called 'I'm Going In.' If I make a mistake, it doesn't mean that something is going terribly wrong. It just means—"

She stops her sentence midair, and she sings, "I am ready to go now, I'm going in, I'm going in, I'm going in." She plays a simple melody on the piano while she sings, and every once in a while, she hits the wrong chord, stops abruptly, and starts over again. But no one cares—they are all crying softly. Her music is painful in its sincerity. Lhasa, visibly trembling, sings like an angel and laughs with every mistake. The pauses are necessary. They provide relief to an overwhelming beautiful song. The audience gets goose bumps listening to her voice, which travels over valleys and plains, dancing with a music that sounds so strange yet feels so familiar. She comes from another place, and here, in this moment, she shares her heart with us.

A year after that performance, Lhasa is diagnosed with breast cancer. She has just finished recording her last album, simply titled "Lhasa." It is by far her best album. No note is in excess, and almost every song speaks of death in one cadence or another. Twenty-one months later, she dies on New Year's Day, and for three days and three nights straight, snow falls.

Her last song.

Outside it is still snowing. I sit in trance, watching the lights, hearing my heart, and sing another one of her melodies:

What kind of heart would a blind man choose
Would a blind man choose
What's better to wear in the dark for love
In the dark for love than a wooden glove

Tied behind your back, tied behind your back
Where its fingers clack, where its fingers clack
What kind of heart would a blind man choose
Would a blind man choose?

It amazes at how one year ago I could even think of ending my life; the cold loneliness I felt then now seems so distant, as if it lies on the other side of a veil to another world. Here, surrounded by lights and song and the kisses of a million tiny snowflakes, I close my eyes and smile in silent gratitude for my beating heart.

CHAPTER 15

THE WASHING ROOM II

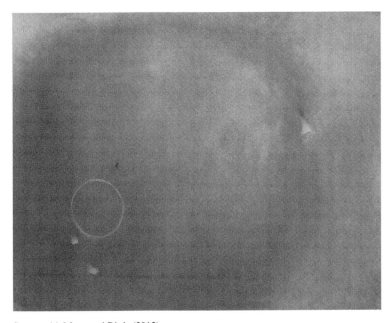

Sunset with Moon and Birds (2012)
Chalk Pastel on Paper
26 in x 18 in

"Sunk in the grass of an empty lot on a spring Saturday, I split the stems of milkweed and thought about ants and peach pits and death and where the world went when I closed my eyes."

— Toni Morrison, *The Bluest Eye*

IN THE TWO YEARS since I became a features writer for The Advocate, I have only visited the building twice: once for initiations and another time to retrieve some clothes I had put there for summer storage. That day I set off the alarm. The police came, and from then on I avoided the building.

Almost year and a half later, on Thursday, February 28, at 4:48 p.m., I arrive at that same house on 21 South Street for a third time to clean the bathroom.

A girl lets me into the building, as I had lost my key. "Thanks for doing this," she says.

"No problem at all," I say. "I should be thanking you for letting me do this."

Once in a while, members of The Advocate have to pay fifty dollars in dues. I already used up most of my spending money that month buying food and liquor for my friends who turned twenty-one, so I asked if there was any other way to compensate for my membership. They gave me three options: sell two copies of the magazine, secure an advertisement, or clean the bathroom.

In the past years I had tried selling magazines to friends and acquaintances, but I ended up just sounding very pretentious and distant, since I had not talked to them since graduation and was writing only to ask for money. Talking to potential sponsors seemed too mentally draining, so naturally, I chose manual labor.

The girl points me to the assortment of cleaning gear gathered in the corner of the bathroom. "Let me know if you need anything else," she says and steps out. I close the door behind me and turn around to take in the scenery.

The bathroom itself is quite small, about the size of a large closet. It has enough space to squeeze in a sink, a small cabinet and a toilet stall. Several layers of dried fluids cover the surfaces of the bathroom. The checkered floor had at some point gleamed white, but now are covered in a fine, crusted brown film which becomes particularly thick near the toilet, at which point it transforms into a sort of compostable bathroom mat.

I check the supplies. The stock includes three spray battles of all-purpose cleaner, a mop, two plastic packages of large yellow durable rubber gloves, a Swiffer duster, two boxes of replacement pads and a large set of paper towels. All brand new.

I pick up the objects one by one. The plastic containing the gloves is smooth and crisp. I open the top and let the gloves slide out. They are too large and run up almost to my elbow, but I feel safe wearing them.

I am at the nail store again, cleaning the bathroom. This time, though, it is different.

Back then I almost never wore gloves. My mom did not either until one day a streak of the callus remover got on her hand without her knowing. It ate through parts of her skin, and by the end of the day a streak of red welts and bumps appeared where the callus remover had stayed. Her hand ached for days. After that, she wore gloves and told me to do the same.

Her method of attaining gloves, however, was not the most sanitary. She saved any used gloves in a box under her station. If she had to clean, she took out a pair, used them a second time and then threw them away. She knew that the State Board would fine her if they found out, but the extra dollars saved was worth the risk of getting caught.

    I could understand my mom's pride in being resourceful, but I felt like it was acceptable to splurge a bit and use the new latex gloves. Still, they often overheated my hands and tore at the most inappropriate times, so I avoided gloves entirely unless I needed to do a pedicure.

    With my hands covered in yellow armor, I proceed with the cleaning ritual. I look among the assortment of bottles and deem the Clorox most suited for the job. Its nozzle is still in the *OFF* position. I twist the cap and squeeze the handle, and it lets out a fine, strong squirt.

    After turning the faucet on, I remember that there are no scrubbing pads. This means I will have to use paper towels. I calculate in my head how much paper I will have to use. Through the gloves I admire the paper with its fine, porous imprints pressed onto every sheet. My parents never understood how Americans could use this paper so lavishly, and here I am committing the inconceivable.

    I tear out about five sheets and crumple them up to make a pad. I feel like I have just done something terrible, but I keep on ripping them out. The sink turns smooth and white again as the pile of soiled paper grows behind me. When the sink is scrubbed down, I flood the surface with water and watch all the flecks of back grime ooze out of the corners and crevices surrounding the faucet—a trick I taught myself over the years. With every flush of water, a new army of green, black, blue and brown flecks emerge from the shadows, slide down the side of the sink and disappear into the drain. Places touched by human hands never fail to turn black with time.

    After the sink comes the toilet. My heart sinks at the thought of having to place my face so close to the rim, but it putters right back up again when I see the toilet brush. The bristles are arranged in a semicircle around the tip of the handle so that I can clean the bowl and the upper rims at the same time. I quickly fall into a solid work cycle: spray the toilet with the cleaner, wet the brush and scrub off the grime, rinse it out, flush the toilet, and repeat as needed. In a few minutes the toilet is sparkling.

My hands aren't even wet yet.

The floor comes next. I place all the materials outside and spray the floor with Clorox. I use more liquid than necessary — it is just so liberating to squirt juice wherever I want. I feel like a child blowing bubbles. After that I wet the mop head. For such a tiny space, I have to rinse and repeat eight times to get all the dirt off. The difference, however, astonishes me: it is as if stage lights have just been turned on to illuminate the floor in its cream-colored glory.

The last thing on the list is to clean the mirror; just as a bedroom does not look tidy until the bed is made, a bathroom does not feel clean until the mirror is spotless. I save this task for the end because it offers the most satisfaction for the least amount of work. All it requires is two sprays of Windex and a quick wipe with a paper towel. In a few seconds, I am done.

I step back and admire my work. I feel like I a nurse who has just given a bath to an old, neglected man. The walls, which can now breathe again, offer their thanks in quiet evening prayers. Then I place the back the cleaning supplies to their original corner and take out the trash, admiring the high-quality plastic bag as I tie together the handles.

After making sure all the lights are off, I stand in front of the alarm, wait for the light to turn green, press the On/Off button until it beeps three times, and then leave, closing the door quietly behind me. I do everything right this time, and the alarm does not sound.

Outside the sun has not yet set. It is only 5:30. With care, I place the trash bag into the bin behind the gym and walk on, my and then during breaks to help out, though now I mostly stick do doing manicures.

Chi Nhung is still working as a pharmacist at the same Walgreens that she started at more than ten years ago. She is very involved with her church and does good every day. I have faith that her three adorable children will grow up to be awesome people. They live in the same subdivision as us, so whenever I go back home I get to play with the babies.

Chi Ti is now thriving in Florida. She has a new job as a management engineer and serves as a big director person for the North Florida Division of the Hospital Corporation of America (NFDHCA). She also got her second masters and now has a long string of letters following her last name (BME, MHA, MSHS). She has a fiancé now. They are happy together—in love too—and I expect that within five years she will have kids of her own.

Those golden shoes broke. I gave the loafers to Chi Ti because they were a tad bit too tight on my feet. The new tennis shoes are still here. I wear them when I go on long bike rides.

Na is in high school now. She's still sweet as always and has grown up to be very cute and good at math. Her mom now owns her own nail store and has a permanent boyfriend who is a good father figure to Na.

I haven't seen any of the people at Oakwood or McLean since I left. My heart goes out to them, and to anyone and everyone who has sunk into darkness, and I hope they are on their way to a warmer, brighter place.

ACKNOWLEDGEMENTS

I am indebted to all those who have supported me through the events of this story and the process of putting it on paper: thank you to my block-mates, Madalyn Bates, Lauren Covalucci, Kalyn Saulsberry and Christina Twicken, for being there; thank you Joey Tran, Jimmy James, Neal Dach, Andrew Woodward, Benjamin Woo, Joe Feghali, Christine An, John Heilbron and Ivan Duralde, for your incredible support; thank you Hojung Lee and Eva Kim, for your prayers; thank you Didar Kul-Mukhammed, Malaya Saldana, James McDowell, Zakiya Haji-Noor, Lynette Osinubi, Jennifer Zhu, Brooke Griffin and Amy Wong, for your friendship, and for reading the original drafts; thank you William, for holding my hand; thank you Amy Wang, my little sister, for staying true, and for your writing; thank you Dr. White-Bateman, Dr. Joan Ford, Dr. Kai, Yolanda Monteiro and Aurora Sanfeliz for the great treatment; thank you Lisa Boes, for being there; thank you Ms. Huie for believing in my writing; thank you Mrs. Nollner for bringing the art out of me; thank you to all the ambulance drivers, taxi drivers, and nurses who gave me so much wisdom; thank you to all my friends from Oakwood and McLean for teaching me so much; thank you Na for teaching me a bit more about love; thank you Chi Nhung and Chi Ti, for being the most amazing sisters I could ever ask for; and lastly, thank you Ba Me, for making me possible. I love you.